How Women Create Success

fab
COLLAB

Tracey Barr • Elena Brennan • Bina Briggs
Victoria Burt • Henriette Danel • Falguni Desai
Debbie Gilbert • Mary Gregory • Enfys Maloney
Andrea L Richards • Bonny Snowdon • Jade Thomas
Lorraine Thomas • Lisa Webb • Hela Wozniak-Kay

First published in Great Britain in 2023 by
Panoma Press Ltd
www.rethinkpress.com
www.panomapress.com

CONTENTS

FOREWORD

Many years ago, when I still worked in the corporate world, I had to collaborate with others in a multitude of ways. I was employed in large and small companies, and in each I was required to liaise with colleagues in my own department and in different departments or business units. It isn't always easy to know how to work with others, especially when you are not part of an official team or there are no clear-cut instructions, and I don't think I was always successful; in fact, in one off-site leadership meeting, I was accused of putting tasks ahead of people. That feedback was upsetting as I saw myself as a people person, but it made me more thoughtful in future interactions and I think I have improved a lot (if you know me, please feel free to confirm or deny that!).

Over the past two decades, I have run two businesses and four brands. There is no way I could have built any of those without collaborating effectively – with virtual team members (never having any employees on my payroll), business partners, joint venture partners, networking colleagues, suppliers… the list goes on. People who are successful in business and in their careers are almost always the ones who not only get along with others but also support them, always looking for and creating mutual opportunities for success. It is a cliché that TEAM stands for Together Everyone Achieves More but it is true, just like many other overused sayings.

When a few of us came up with the concept of this book, it sounded fun to collaborate on a book about collaboration. All the authors are members of a special community called Sister Snog, which fosters collaboration and mutual support, so they know a lot about how to create success by working in partnership with others. It was daunting, however, to find a way to weave the wisdom of so many businesswomen together while also meeting their diverse needs. We – the authors – see collaboration as one of the key skills for success, so the stakes were high and we wanted to produce something special.

We needn't have worried: the project ended up being much more enjoyable and valuable than any of us had anticipated. I am impressed by the various perspectives on this important topic, and the heart-warming and creative stories studded throughout the book. As you read, you will discover different angles and insights on how to develop this necessary skill. You will find yourself nodding in agreement, shaking your head in amazement and excited to try new ideas as fast as possible. Whether you think you are already good at working with others or you feel it is not one of your strengths, please know that the authors believe in you. We have poured our best insights into these chapters with love and care. We all wish you success and fun as you create some 'fab collabs' in your life and business.

Mindy Gibbins-Klein, Award-Winning International Speaker, Author and Entrepreneur

PART I

Defining true collaboration

CHAPTER 1

What Is Collaboration?

LORRAINE THOMAS

Let me start with a few ideas about what collaboration is not. It's not working together on the same project. Bear with me. I'll come back to this. It's not visual or used to describe things that look or sound the same. It's not an individual effort. It's not merely an exchange of ideas.

My take on collaboration starts with the difference between marriage and cohabitation. In marriage, the words 'I do' are defining. They are the foundation of the ultimate collaboration. Often, there is a lot of thought, agony, discussion, tears, prayer and soul-searching before those words are uttered publicly in front of family and friends. The impact of saying 'I do' and then realising you don't can be huge, both legally and emotionally. My point is that living together is a much easier deal. It's a similar soul-searching exercise, but cohabiting offers a swifter exit minus the red tape. Collaboration ties everyone in on a far deeper level than simply being part of a team that is getting on with the job and meeting expectations. Think of it as a marriage of minds. A communion between shared values. A desire to work together in harmony like a horse and carriage.

In the simplest of terms, collaboration achieves something over and above what one person can achieve in isolation. We've all heard the phrase, 'The sum of the parts is greater than the whole.' Amen to that. If there's a shared purpose, the end result is often greater and more meaningful than the original expectation. The beauty of collaboration rests in the journey, which inevitably leads to something bigger, bolder and brighter than expected. Possibilities unfold.

Contributions don't need to be split fifty-fifty. They just need to have a parity and a sense of equality for the magic to occur. The different skill sets, gifts and attributes in varying measures are what make a collaboration pop. Rather like your favourite curry; the kick generally comes from the smallest chilli pepper.

I mentioned that collaboration is not simply working together as a team; it runs far deeper than that. You must share the same purpose and end goal. It's teamwork personified as every collaborator is there out of choice rather than design. You are called to collaboration, not collared. True collaborations in today's connected world are not restricted by geography; you could be halfway across the world from someone with whom you are working on a project with a shared purpose.

As a small business owner, I see collaboration as the enrichment of others through a shared mission. It starts from within. Those that share your vision and want to work alongside you will stand out and you will gravitate towards them. Collaboration has two *l*'s that must align, move in the same direction and have a common purpose.

Defining the various forms of collaboration

I'm a collaborator by nature; it's my default setting. It's not always easy though, as the following examples illustrate.

Contractors on-site

Working with contractors can be hard work and complicated at the best of times. Different agendas can lead to misunderstanding. This makes collaboration tricky as more layers need unwrapping before a shared purpose is revealed.

In my experience, the contractor wants to complete the job in the fastest time. They want to get in and out with the least amount of cost. They want to do a good job for future recommendation, but knowing that the developer depends on their expertise, they often believe they hold *all* the cards. The developer, on the other hand, will want a builder who is consistent, exceptional at their work, cost-effective and available to return should there be any snags following completion. They hold the cash cards.

Each party holding a deck of cards that doesn't necessarily align with the other is not a great recipe for collaboration. This is due to an underlying lack of trust – one of the key components to a collaborative flow. The contractor needs to trust the developer will pay on time. The developer needs to trust the contractor will not rip them off.

If you can pinpoint the barriers, you can always find a way around them. I've achieved this by playing to my contractors' strengths: allowing them to make choices without me, demonstrating trust; rewarding for early completion; explaining my business purpose, what we do and why it's important to produce good work on time and at a reasonable cost. Often, knowing my business, View From My Window, houses vulnerable and disadvantaged people and helps to get young people onto the property ladder, encourages contractors to see us from an individual perspective and they want to help. This means I level out the playing field. They have a choice. Buy into my business and its values. Or not. Before collaboration comes commitment. That's when the collaboration starts and other things you have in common appear.

Mentees

Mentees have high expectations, aspirations and dreams. They often underestimate how difficult it is in property to get deals over the line. Managing expectations can be high maintenance and expertise alone does not cut it. They have to trust you. Once they do this, the relationship is ideal for collaboration. I would go so far as to say that without it, no one wins.

The shared goal is to get your mentee onto the property ladder or owning their own portfolio. A mutual goal. A shared mission. This is where a collaborative approach has to come into play. My goal is to lift others and help them to grow and flourish. I set out the ABC steps I'm willing to take so they can add the XYZ. Together, we create the alphabet of success. It's a collaborative journey based on trust, shared values and mutual understanding – and it works.

Developers and investors

Coming together to learn and share so others can grow is the ultimate collaboration. This is why I see beyond the competitive nature of other developers and investors. The right competitors represent my best collaborators as our shared differences reveal how similar we are.

No two property developers or investors are mirror copies of each other. We each tend to specialise in a particular property strategy, and while strategies can cross over, they can also cross-pollinate. As a result, together we can innovate and create something explosive, as we often do.

My business partner

Partnerships truly flourish when both parties join the project with a collaborative approach and bring a complementary set of skills, wisdom, know-how and knowledge. When my business partner and I started the partnership, I was a carer for my father, but I came with lots of business development experience. She was a successful businesswoman with extensive experience in the social care space.

Her business lacked the increasing number of homes needed to house the young people that were coming out of supervised care. I stepped in to help her look for those homes and later down the line bought accommodation with her. We had three things in common: neither of us had any experience in property; we each had a huge desire to house disadvantaged young adults in decent accommodation; we were each driven by our passion to make money and run a successful business. These three things led to a solid collaboration. She brings attributes that I don't bring and vice versa. We are achieving far more together than we ever could alone.

Tenants

In order for our business to thrive, we have to enter a partnership with tenants that goes beyond the payment of rent on time. The tenant wants a decent roof over their head with affordable rent and we want a happy tenant who loves where they live. Trust and respect are built between the two parties standing together. Our tenants have big dreams and being a collaborative landlord is key to supporting them.

Summary

Good collaboration requires different skill sets all moving within a millimetre of each other to achieve a common goal. The team needs to have depth and breadth and a sprinkle of magic, but it is better to have one person that you connect with on many levels than 200 people who you don't connect with at all and who could therefore hold you back. If you are fortunate enough to find the right partnership, this will underpin any future collaboration. Alter your mindset and step away from 'I can do it better' and into 'We can do it *much* better'. No woman is an island. No one person has all the answers.

TIPS FOR COLLABORATION

1. Spell it right

Look for two *l*'s in the word. If it's spelt with one *l*, then it definitely isn't collaboration. There is no *i* in team but there is in collaboration. Embrace the *i* because you need individual commitment to make the group effort take flight. There is always a leader in a group and that leader needs to know how to bring

together others to create something explosive.
No one of us can be or is as smart as all of us.

2. Dig deeper

You will know when you're on the road to
collaboration because your innermost desires
and intuition come alive and you start to share
those feelings. Your awareness changes to
incorporate the others in your partnership and
that's reciprocated.

3. If it feels like hard work then it probably is

Collaboration done well should feel like light
work, enrichment and a real gift. Remember,
you are called to collaboration, not collared.

4. The sum of the parts is far greater

Those big dreams become real when they're
broken down into bite-sized chunks and
shared with like-minded people who then
create collaborative processes or collective
moments of genius.

5. Surround yourself with greatness

Working with someone who sees what they
do as no more than a job or task might
reduce your world and shrink your vision.
Co-operating is not collaborating. Stay among
those who continue to make your dreams
scare you because they are so big.

6. **Lay your cards on the table from the get-go**

   Outline your purpose, objectives and understanding of the project. Clear up grey areas that could be misinterpreted.

7. **Listen**

   Listen carefully to the message when you are setting out the goals; it is so much deeper than the words alone. Don't just read the words from the other parties and take those as a done deal.

8. **Monitor your thoughts and feelings**

   Clear the destructive feelings from within and show up constructively, ready to align your ideas and produce something bigger than you.

Lorraine Thomas is an award-winning property developer, mentor and socially conscious landlord. She is an outspoken advocate who believes in property with purpose and people before profit, a giant-thinking, risk-taking visionary who's shaking up the sector and becoming a sought-after voice.

In 2016 Lorraine took a leap from her career in business development in the legal sector when she landed a role procuring rental properties for disadvantaged young adults. This was a defining moment which led to her buying and developing properties from the ground up and renting to high-risk and vulnerable tenants.

Today, Lorraine mentors other budding developers and is on a mission to create a new breed of socially conscious landlords who combine commercial savviness with a social conscience.

🌐 www.viewfrommywindow.co.uk

in www.linkedin.com/in/lorrainethomasview

◙ www.instagram.com/view_from_my_window__

CHAPTER 2

Collaboration Is Inherent

BINA BRIGGS

When I was presented with the subject, I went round in circles for days, thinking of all the grandiose ways I could define its meaning and application in business. Then I just let it be, and suddenly I had an epiphany: collaboration is as ancient as womankind; it is inherent, a way of life for all of us, so why am I making it such a difficult subject to write about?

From the beginning of time, human beings have depended on each other, forming families, communities, tribes or nations. Collaboration in its simplest form is about working together to gain mutual benefit, whether that is within a social, personal or commercial context. It is the fabric of life. It is about sharing skills, knowledge and expertise for a common goal. As women, we are at the heart of it all.

Although it is said that it's a man's world, for me, women are the powerhouse. Starting with our own families, we realise that everything we achieve is through collaboration with family members, neighbours and friends. The same principle applies in the business world, because women are natural collaborators: we share our dreams, take action together and make our goals happen with flair, gentle persuasion, glamour and often with a steely determination.

The fundamental element of collaboration for me is the desire for success for all parties concerned. The other key component is being me in every aspect. People want transparency, trustworthiness, integrity and genuineness in others in any collaboration. In business, collaboration is defined as a practice whereby individuals work together with a common purpose to achieve business benefit.

As a woman entrepreneur and having earlier had a corporate career, I have seen how women bring new perspectives on getting things done. When we look a little deeper into any business or organisation that has women as decision makers or that has realised the great value of having women with a voice in their teams, there is a softer edge to the way the business is conducted. That doesn't mean we are weak; it just means that we know much more is achieved through the ethos of sharing, working together with a gentle touch towards a common goal. Collaboration is entwined in every aspect of my business and life in general.

As a result of the Covid pandemic of 2020/2021, the world has realised the severe impact of isolation, and how we all depend on each other, whether on a personal or commercial level. When the world opened up again for all of us from late 2021 onwards, collaboration became even more important as the key to success in every part of our lives. We may label it differently in each situation – 'networking', 'working together' etc – but in the end, it comes down to collaboration.

Collaboration across families, communities, tribes from ancient times

Collaboration has to start from me. My family, culture and my personal life made me who I am, before I embarked on my corporate life as an entrepreneur and a successful published author. Women tend to be nurturers – and that comes through in every mode of life. Women have played a crucial part in it all.

As a Hindu, I was brought up in the traditional environment of family life, extended families and community. Women have played a pivotal part in my life, from my maternal grandmother, the matriarch KamalaBaa, to my mum and my aunties, my cousins, sisters, sisters-in-law and nieces. Each one is a diamond, a strong woman in her own way, not only achieving her dreams but contributing to society and the world at large – and how did they achieve all this? With a collaborative mindset.

During my working life in the corporates – as a data clerk in Court Line, in BT Computing and as head of HR for London Luton Airport – teams mattered in every way, both internal and external. Each of the organisations valued teamwork as a recognised way of existing. Collaboration was at the heart of it all.

As an entrepreneur at Plain Talking HR, collaboration has been the key to my success. Networking has been fundamental to my business, and the women-based networking organisations I have been involved in have been my lifeline. I was a little sceptical when I joined a women's networking group, Women in Business Network (WIBN). I had forgotten that we care about our fellow women, that we are supportive and form genuine bonds quickly. I was reassured when this became clear from the beginning. Women recognise that we are all in it together and that if we collaborate and reach out to others who can help us and whom we can support, all of us are better off. We tend to be nurturers in nature and that comes through in every mode of life.

When talking about women networking groups, WIBN taught me the way to connect with other women and the importance of having the mindset of giving before receiving. Women of all ages, backgrounds and expertise suddenly became my go-to experts, sounding boards, collaborators and friends. We genuinely looked out for each other. Under the guardianship of Louise Yexley, I learnt a lot about other professions, strategies for business and techniques to be a better collaborator.

From there, my life opened up to possibilities and connections I had previously thought impossible. Debbie Gilbert, marketing genius extraordinaire, took me under her wing and my business started to fly. Debbie not only helped me gain exposure on social media but she also introduced me to the many fabulous women of substance she knew, two stellar connections in particular who have made an astronomical difference to my life: Mindy Gibbins-Klein and Hela Wozniak-Kay.

Mindy Gibbins-Klein is a TEDx speaker and founder of the multi-award-winning brand The Book Midwife®. Mindy supported me in bringing my book, *The Red Thread*, to life. Without her, my dream would have remained a dream. The book is about strong women and it was brought to life by women. The publicity has all been managed by women. The book has opened up opportunities I could have never imagined, and it's brought even more amazing women into my life – women who have united for common causes. This year in 2022 is the fiftieth anniversary of the Ugandan Asians expulsion. Due to my background, I have had the privilege of being interviewed by Dolar Vasani for one of her podcasts;[1] Dolar and her family were among the thousands of people of Indian origin expelled from Uganda. I have also become part of a group of wonderful women keeping

---

1   Vasani, D, 'Commemorating the 50th anniversary of the expulsion of Ugandan Asians' Expulsion@50 (no date), https://anchor.fm/expulsion50, accessed 6 December 2022

history alive by holding exhibitions of the events and lives of the Ugandan Asians diaspora in the UK.[2][3]

This chapter wouldn't have been written without Hela Wozniak-Kay and Sister Snog. Nothing I say here can do them justice. I had become aware of Sister Snog through its exquisite name and its unique presence on social media. Its flamboyance is Hela's personification of Sisterliness, the ethos of genuine female entrepreneurship. The Sisters are all selected by Hela on the basis of showing the qualities of being collaborators, supporting and nurturing each other, giving and serving; of having strong values of integrity, trust, honesty, innovation, inspiration and entrepreneurship; and of wanting to have fun. Each event is curated with the highest creativity by Hela, with the help of Sisters specialising in the areas required for the event to be memorable. Every single detail is taken care of to achieve perfection and create a wow factor.

Summary

My dear reader, you will have now realised that I have a lot to be grateful to the women around me for, and I cannot see that changing for the rest of my life. I hope that some of my experiences as an award-winning businesswoman, a published author and a woman who

---

2   Uganda Asians – Living History, www.instagram.com/ugandanasians, accessed 7 December 2022

3   Once Upon A Time 50 Years Ago - Uprooted Ugandian Asians UK, www.instagram.com/uprooted50yearsago, accessed 9 March 2023

has lived and travelled well may strike a chord with you and help you.

TIPS FOR COLLABORATION

1. Be yourself

First and foremost, be yourself. As Maya Angelou said, 'You alone are enough, you have nothing to prove to anybody'[4] and 'Your legacy is every life you touch.'[5] Always show up as you, and be genuine – being the shining star you are will always stand you in good stead. People want to see the integrity in you when they meet you.

2. Make sure you are in alignment

For me, the next important thing is to check if the other person's values match my own. Are we aligned in our thoughts and actions? Because, as you know, people 'buy' people; they need to know they can trust you and that they like you before they engage with your

---

4   Winfrey, O, 'What Oprah Knows for Sure About Being a Supportive Friend', *The Oprah Magazine* (September 2017), www.oprah.com/inspiration/what-oprah-knows-for-sure-about-being-a-supportive-friend, accessed 7 December 2022

5   Angelou, M (@DrMayaAngelou) 'You alone are enough. You have nothing to prove to anybody' (18 July 2021), https://twitter.com/drmayaangelou/status/1416760512302485507?lang=en, accessed 7 December 2022

business. I ask myself, 'Do I feel comfortable with them?' 'Can I see them sharing and understanding my vision?' If I don't feel right with any of it, time and experience has proved to me that it will not work. I listen to my inner voice, my intuition. The money or the gains to be had from any collaboration are not enough to outweigh any discontent and pain. If it doesn't feel right, I've found it's better to let it go at the outset. I cannot be everyone's choice and that is OK, just as not everyone will be my choice.

3. Be clear about your reasons

In business, be crystal clear about why you need to collaborate. Who would be the best person or company to help you? Have you clearly agreed what you would both bring to the collaboration and how this would be achieved? It may take you a number of attempts to find the right collaborator. This is where your database of contacts and networks comes into play. Ask advice from your trusted sources and research the referrals. Check out LinkedIn, for instance, and don't settle for second best.

Once you've agreed to go ahead with any collaboration, it's critical that you have the project plan in place and that this covers everything that matters, especially costs and timescales. Who is going to track progress? How and how frequently are they going to do that? What contingencies do you have in place in case anything goes wrong or in the event that there is slippage on delivery?

4. Enjoy yourself

Finally, enjoy what you do. Collaboration is about positive outcomes, about success, progress, innovation, happiness and celebration. Coming back full circle, life is for living and, whatever we do, sharing the successes with the people we have achieved our goals with is the proof in the pudding. Awards, accolades and celebrations all add up to the sweetest outcomes of any collaboration.

Bina Briggs is an award-winning female entrepreneur, and an expert in HR. After a long corporate career, Bina has focused on delivering her plain-talking outsourced service to her clients, who love her pragmatic approach. Bina is a volunteer for many charities and organisations, especially those supporting women's issues.

Author of the bestselling book *The Red Thread*, Bina arrived in this country as a refugee from Uganda in 1972. Her book shares an invaluable message of love, kindness and support, and celebrates the collaboration, strength, determination, resilience, tenderness, gratitude and humour learnt through the life lessons, failures, friendships and successes experienced mainly by women.

Bina is proud to be a member of Sister Snog.

 www.plaintalkinghr.com

🌐 www.theredthreadbook.co.uk

CHAPTER 3

The Many Faces Of Collaboration

ANDREA L RICHARDS

Collaboration is personalities, traits, thoughts and mindsets combining to create something that is far greater than any one person can do on their own. It has many forms, whether it be collaborating professionally to achieve a greater goal or collaborating on a more personal level to ensure goals are met without sacrificing mental fortitude.

Collaboration is essential to long-term survival – after all, cavemen had to collaborate to find their next meal and forage the right foods – and to any entrepreneur or future businesswoman. You cannot learn something from nothing; it is necessary to assimilate knowledge from others to use for yourself and teach to other people. Efficient collaboration can solve many of the world's problems. It can address race issues through the moulding and connecting of diverse cultures and an understanding that, even though each individual has their own identity, together we are more than the sum of our parts.

Collaboration can also find answers to many of the world's technological problems. Many minds working together is infinitely better than one mind working on one problem, which can raise issues of resources and time. Collaboration can improve many aspects of an economy and help countries in crisis. The UK and western countries are currently providing support to Ukraine, who have the upper hand in the war against Russia, a country known for preventing the spread of Rome, the Ottomans, Napoleon and Germany during World War II. The UK has bailed out other countries economically, preventing disastrous collapses of economic centres and providing stability. All of this has been achieved through collaboration.

Collaboration is putting aside personal pride for personal growth. For some, it is not easy to work with others, especially if you are opinionated or do not generally work well as part of a team. Being able to put aside the need to do everything yourself shows personal development; it can help the progress of any project and facilitate goals being met. For others, collaboration means family. If collaboration is done well between family members, it can bring out the best in them, allowing an individual to flourish in a peaceful environment and having a positive impact on the trajectory of their life progress.

Lastly, collaboration is communication, a skill that can be learnt and improved on and one that many people take for granted. Without good communication, you cannot have a good collaboration. Communication is more than speaking; it is talking about how you feel. To truly be in sync with a collaborative partner, you will need to be able to communicate each person's needs.

The life stages of collaboration

Collaboration has been at the forefront of many aspects of my life. It has not only enabled me to overcome difficulties, but it has also allowed me to flourish in a difficult period both economically and personally.

My first form of major collaboration was with my mum, a woman to whom I owe a great amount of success. After having a child at the tender age of fifteen, I was still in school and a future was not clearly paved out. Although at the time collaboration was tough, especially for a teenager with the stresses of GCSEs looming over her as well as the ever-menacing teenage angst, my mum helped me greatly. I would take my child to nursery, then go to work doing my nine-to-five, and she would ensure my child was picked up safely and looked after while I continued my studies towards becoming a qualified accountant after the working day had finished. This has no doubt influenced the individual I am today, both personally and in business.

My second major collaboration was with my employers. After many conversations with my then bosses, we came up with a solution that would benefit both parties. I demonstrated my fantastic work ethic while they paid for and allowed me to attend college after work. This enabled me to cement my knowledge and lit up the path to the accountancy career I have wanted since I was a nine-year-old child. It allowed me to create the foundations and principles necessary to begin the journey of self-employment. Extensive collaboration with my employers has given me opportunities to look at unique styles of leadership and combine a mixture of them to create my own, which has served me to this day.

My third collaboration was with my partner. Being a mother, working full-time and studying can paralyse those who are not prepared for sleepless nights and those who are unable to graft to get what they need. I collaborated with my partner through effectively communicating my needs and my vision for the future. The days were long: the majority exceeded eighteen-hour workdays, seven days a week. My partner was the one to look after my children, ensuring they were fed, watered, educated and disciplined, while I carved out a future for myself and my family. Through this collaboration, I started my own business as an accountancy practice owner.

Before starting a limited company, what had initially seemed like the misfortune of being made redundant in the international law firm I worked in turned out to be my saving grace: it allowed me to begin the process of working for myself. I was fortunate enough to come across, collaborate with and work for five separate small businesses and, through intercompany collaboration, they introduced me to many other small business owners who required my business acumen and skills. This enhanced my network and helped me to expand my business.

Through all of the different collaborations I have had the pleasure of coming across, and despite the hard work, blood, sweat, tears and sleep deprivation, I was able to create a business that is now flourishing. It is essential to collaborate and communicate with my clients to build understanding and trust. This way, I can anticipate their needs and communicate effectively to get them where they need to be to achieve their dream goals.

Within this, there are also elements of inter-client collaborations. As a trusted entity, we provide our clients with the best sources of information and networking opportunities. After we hosted a successful client networking event, many clients met each other and began collaborating on projects which would not have been possible if the initial level of trust that is needed to function, such an event, had not been there in the first place.

My team is a crucial resource to my business. I collaborate extensively and daily with staff, meeting their needs and understanding how to get the best out of them through effective communication. In turn, my staff will continue to deliver the trusted service I offer my clients. I understand that the team are the lifeblood of the office as the day-to-day operations go through them, and collaborating with them is essential to the maintenance and growth of the company.

Summary

I am sure you have heard the time-old adage: it is not about *what* you know but about *who* you know. This holds true. It is said that you only need to know four people to have access to the network of the world. Connecting with individuals who know others within your industry or who need someone to help them within your industry can present untold opportunities, and this does not necessarily come from the education you receive but from the people you work and collaborate with. Your network is your net worth.

TIPS FOR COLLABORATION

1. Learn to put pride behind you

Pride is an extremely healthy trait to have but can sometimes hinder growth, especially when collaborating with individuals. Although there is something special in saying 'I have made it on my own', no billionaire got to where they are now without collaboration from one or more other entities. I understand more minds means more friction points, but it also opens you up to more thought processes and a wider skill set, which makes collaboration invaluable.

2. Go outside of your comfort zone

Growth does not come from being inside your comfort zone. You need to be uncomfortable to grow. This can come in the form of collaborating with people you would not normally consider speaking to and may not think of collaborating with initially. Individuals working together with the same ideologies can create something amazing but not necessarily something new; when individuals who are different come together, the opportunity to create something new and exciting arises.

3. Listen twice as much as you talk

Knowledge is power, and finding learning opportunities wherever possible, especially on subjects you are not familiar with, is the key to personal growth and success. Collaborating with those that are 'smarter' than you opens you up to different avenues of growth and learning and allows you to absorb material that you would not ordinarily be around; in other words, you do not know what you do not know. We have two ears and one mouth, and applying active listening skills instead of jumping in on a subject you are not familiar with can work to your advantage.

4. Use the tools you have available

This does not necessarily mean to use a hammer on a nail, but to use your circle and your contacts as well as the family and friends around you to get the best out of what you can do and reach your potential. Your family and friends should be your first point of call as they will want what is best for you, and allowing others to help or delegating work is a strong sign of leadership and attracts others to collaborating with you. From there, use your network to achieve more collaborations that will help further your goals.

Andrea L Richards is the founder and finance director of a multi-award-winning, modern and digital accountancy practice – Accounts Navigator Associates Limited. The company is based in Waltham Abbey, Essex and works with clients both locally and nationwide.

For the last twenty years, Andrea has partnered with individuals, entrepreneurs and businesses to take control of their finance function to maximise their profit and minimise their tax, and help grow their business using management accounts. With fantastic levels of communication and drawing from her thirty-two years of accounting and business experience, Andrea makes sure all her clients understand their figures so they make wise and fruitful business decisions, and will never be left in the dark when it comes to tax.

🌐 www.accountsnavigator.com

in www.linkedin.com/in/andrea-l-richards-a0075b41

✉ andrea@accountsnavigator.com

PART 2

The Essential ingredients for successful collaboration

CHAPTER 4

Trust Is The Cornerstone For All Partnerships

FALGUNI DESAI

Collaboration, for me, is the mutually beneficial act of working together with a common purpose towards a shared goal. The word is derived from the Latin word *collaborare*, which means 'to work with' – and that is the sweet spot of the idea of collaboration.

I believe the essence of working with someone is mutual trust. Once there is trust many wonderful things follow. Such as, a supportive environment, open communication, enhanced motivation, light bulb moments of inspiration, genius innovations and an evolving success story.

Observable attributes of successful collaboration include, but are not limited to:[6]

- **Shared motivation** – having a common understanding and purpose of the intended goals

- **Participation** – ensuring that all team members have the opportunity to be involved

- **Teamworking** – enabling behaviours which result in group harmony, allowing good relationships to be cultivated

- **Decision making** – providing the right structure to expedite decisions when necessary

- **Information handling** – implementing information-sharing policies and processes to ensure the right data is available to all relevant parties at the right time

- **Open Mindset** – being open to and seeking out new possibilities

- **Negotiation** – having a mechanism to enable healthy debate to reach consensus

- **Proactivity** – create a culture of planning ahead and formulating alternatives in advance rather than reacting after the fact

---

6   Institute for Collaborative Working, 'What is Collaborative Working?' (no date), https://instituteforcollaborativeworking.com/About-ICW/What-is-Collaborative-Working, accessed 6 December 2022

When project stakeholders combine key skills, processes and the organisational structure, this results in active collaboration. Benefits of active collaboration may include:

- Cooperation between team leads, supervisors and managers to create coherent tactical ways of working

- Unrestricted resource, data, skills, knowledge and information sharing

- Solid working relationships providing structure to the collaborative process

- Trust, respect and mutual appreciation for roles and responsibilities

When all the elements fall into place, results start to emerge and blossom, often surprisingly quicker than expected. A true collaboration will *take you up the mountain*.

Why trust is vital for successful collaboration

Collaboration for me as a business coach is about working with open-minded, talented and ambitious business owners who are experts in their field. The best collaboration occurs when there is a shift from us working *in* the business to working *on* the business. This gives the client the freedom to think more and do less.

Deep listening, together with an analytical mind, helps business owners find clarity: from 'monkey mind' entrepreneurs who have a million good ideas but are too restless or confused to make them a reality to traditional family businesses. By building trust and listening, true collaboration can embed tried-and-tested strategies that are tailored to client objectives.

The art of collaboration takes on many guises. I would like to share an example of a client I worked with: a family business that had been successful for two decades was being handed over to the next generation, which required a new way of thinking and a commitment to maintaining the essence of a family business. Collaboration led to an amazing transformation and a new way to steer the ship.

If true collaboration is to succeed, it is crucial that the needs of the client are set out at the beginning. There has to be full disclosure. People usually start their own business, or join a family business, for a lifestyle change and, most importantly, to enjoy what they are doing. Open discussion confirmed that this was the aspiration for my client. By understanding the common purpose and key objectives, the collaboration base was established. They aligned their personal goals with their business goals, providing clarity and focus on formulating both a life plan and a business plan.

All businesses have five key areas: sales, marketing, operations, finance and admin, and people management. By identifying the order of priority in which each area is addressed, the challenges can be highlighted. My client made sure priorities were clear, then, every three months, put together a plan with a proposed timeline. They worked consistently on the plan by breaking down the tasks into manageable chunks, which resulted in big improvements.

My client knew that if you want to collaborate but do not communicate, progress is hindered. They arranged regular meetings to shine a light on the work in progress as well as to maintain accountability. As the plan got underway, they identified benchmarks to consistently measure the results, ensuring any changes were picked up quickly. If the results were not improving, they investigated where changes were needed. Across the board, the killer nugget is good time management. Effective delegation, daily time-blocking and allowing interruptions only in an emergency made a dramatic difference to my client. By getting the systems right, testing and measuring everything and sharing the outcomes, they put themselves ahead of their competitors.

Another essential ingredient for collaboration is being available and accessible. A business does not stand still between coach and owner meetings. Being available to the client at short notice if required is part of an open relationship and greatly valued. The reward comes from seeing their professional and personal development, which, in my client's case, was apparent in their growth in confidence and their ability to handle difficult conversations and situations.

Collaboration requires an open-minded approach to the fluidity of the business, the recognition that changes happen internally and externally, and the awareness that there is flexibility in every situation. This understanding is steering my client's company towards a structure where a managing director can eventually run the day-to-day business, giving the owner the option to focus on strategy and growth, take a passive income or sell.

Another area where trust is key to collaboration is networking. As we know, networking is a slow burn. We need to sow the seeds to create a garden, or why not think of it as an orchard with bigger opportunities? Building a meaningful network takes time. Find a place to meet like-minded people, your tribe, that you feel at home with. Collaborations do not happen overnight; you have to be out there, show up at meetings, be present and start building bonds that open doors. Make sure you reciprocate by sharing knowledge, making introductions or contributing in some way.

To collaborate, you need to find the people that you can build a long-lasting relationship with. You may already know them through other connections, or you may get to meet them through a networking group. Networking should be part of your plan. There are many opportunities for an individual to join in-person or virtual groups and be connected with a global audience. Always make sure you find one person you like the look of at every event. Having joined a women's network over two years ago, the best part of my work has come through referrals from the network.

Nobody can fly solo. As a sole business owner, it can sometimes be lonely unless you collaborate with someone. Becoming well known in your network will result in new business. One such client had been running her business for five years, had taken it as far as she could and realised she needed an outside perspective. We initially focused on improving her time management, balancing her workload, improving her financial reporting and identifying her target market. This gave her clarity and the headspace to focus on other areas. She was also able to take weekends off. Having stopped spinning plates, she is more focused and able to take regular breaks. Her client base has doubled, and she has made a number of introductions to me.

Summary

Collaboration is never one-sided. The beauty is we are all being each other's ambassadors. If you are a solo plate-spinner, find someone to collaborate with, someone with whom you can be mutual guides. My experience of working with my clients is based on collaboration and sharing skills. You will spin less plates, end up doing less and gaining more. Collaboration is a journey where like minds go on an adventure with a common purpose that leads to a beautiful result that neither of you could have envisaged.

TIPS FOR COLLABORATION

1. Trust

The key to success in any relationship is trust. It is also important to listen, remember, be interested and interesting. Trust and intuition go together; it is not possible to build a relationship overnight. Find like-minded people, win them over and nurture the ones you resonate with.

2. Find a balance

It is not easy to own and run a business; there is always so much to do and it can get overwhelming and feel like a lonely existence, but firefighting and spinning plates should not be the norm. Most business owners I meet aim to find a way to manage a successful business *and* enjoy their personal life – that all-too-familiar dilemma of finding a healthy work-life balance.

3. Exercise regularly

Wellbeing is at the heart of being able to run a sustainable business without burnout. As businesswomen, or indeed as women, this should be non-negotiable. This means ensuring our health regime is part of our daily routine and woven into the working week. As clichéd as it may sound, without our health, we have nothing.

Find something that you enjoy doing that has movement – walking, swimming, Pilates, dancing, cycling, yoga. There are so many choices. One of my clients enjoys Thai boxing, another loves tai chi – both are busy women but ensure they do not miss their regular sessions. As we know, regular exercise has many health benefits.

4. Sleep

The importance of getting good quality sleep cannot be underestimated. The effects of long-term sleep deprivation can be dangerous and eventually impact your wellbeing.

5. Nourish yourself

One more tip on wellness: dehydration and an unhealthy diet result in tiredness and brain fog, which will ultimately affect your concentration, quality of work and productivity.

6. Have fun

Collaboration is also about having fun. Why is it important to have fun? If there is no fun or laughter, it will just be another task you have to complete; if you are having fun, it will not feel like work. You and those around you will be more productive and engaged. Ensure that you are also having fun outside of work. Plan ahead, be a social butterfly and have things to look forward to. Once in a while, paint the town red.

Falguni Desai is an experienced business growth coach with twenty years' legal experience with a rich and colourful client base. She is committed to helping business owners realise what they set out to do by improving cash flow and profit, spending their time where they add the most value, leveraging the capability of their teams and building a resilient business.

Falguni is an open and enthusiastic coach full of passion for what she does. Working with integrity and empathy, she believes that business, like life, should be fun and fulfilling. She is committed to learning and sharing her knowledge and experience with those around her to help them grow and transform.

🌐 www.actioncoach.co.uk/coaches/falguni-desai

in www.linkedin.com/in/falguni-desai-173a2984

✉ falgunidesai@actioncoach.com

CHAPTER 5

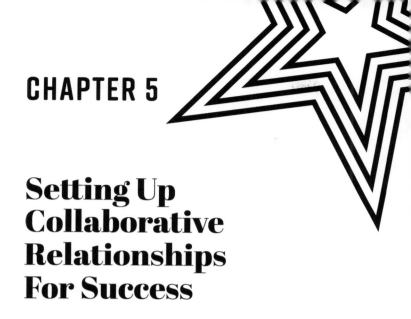

Setting Up Collaborative Relationships For Success

MARY GREGORY

I admit I love collaborating. Working in the world of coaching and developing leaders, I am lucky to have the chance to frequently team up with clients, fellow coaches and facilitators. Collaboration to me is an enriching way to work with others that gives access to solutions we would otherwise not encounter. It is a source of personal growth and contributes to business success. It doesn't necessarily happen naturally. Even if we are gregarious by nature, each of us has our own personality and idiosyncrasies. To ensure collaboration works, we need to set the relationship up through giving it conscious time and attention.

The 'new normal' of business is one of constant, fast-paced change. A collaborative approach in this world builds leadership and business resilience, and increases creativity and innovation. Multileveled and complex challenges require more than simplistic, black-and-white solutions. Leading a modern business requires us to think deeply and harness the diverse resources that collaboration offers.

Traditionally, the number of followers someone can generate has been a measure of leadership, but nowadays leaders don't need to be surrounded by those who always say yes; they need to create fellowship based on collaborative relationships. Better to work with others who'll stretch your thinking, build and challenge ideas, and co-create initiatives which might not have been thought of otherwise. This ensures the growth of the individuals involved as well as their businesses and, in my experience, it is a skill women in business are naturally inclined towards. Such alliances build communities receptive to change, where joint ownership and responsibility give access to a range of resources that would otherwise be out of reach.

A client I recently worked with, a business leader who faced enormous cost cuts, observed, 'The way we get through this is by letting go of our individual agenda and putting the focus on our collective leadership responsibility. It's the purpose our whole division serves that must take priority.' Wise words, yet this is often easier said than done. From what I've observed in business, at times of change some can put their own agenda to one side for the greater good, while others struggle to do this. Lack of self-awareness and self-management result in egos taking over, and all sorts of behavioural games and dynamics emerge which risk sabotaging a collaborative approach.

Using a structure and framework for successful collaboration

Working collaboratively requires a level of consciousness and intentionality which takes personal energy, commitment, insight and motivation. This varies from one person to the next, and it's not just about an individual. How well collaboration works depends on the dynamics of the business leaders involved – how they interact can enable or harm the process.

This is further impacted by the pressure the pace of change creates. I've seen leaders wanting to work well together, but the demands of the situation they face trigger the human reaction of jumping immediately into action. Little thought is given to how they could approach a situation, and not enough time is spent on establishing how they will work together and what successful collaboration would look like for them. Action is taken based on assumptions, which increases the risk of misunderstandings, breakdown and, potentially, failure.

Fortunately, you can overcome this and ensure whatever collaboration you embark upon is set up and maintained as a constructive relationship with good communication. Firstly, you need to slow down to speed up. Why do I say this? I've already acknowledged the propensity, particularly in the business world, to get into the action quickly, but when it comes to working collaboratively, this urgency to get the job done needs to be paused for a moment to ensure the foundations for an effective relationship are put in place.

Think of a time when you had to make something. It could be anything from cake to a piece of flat-pack furniture. Imagine jumping in without taking time to read the instructions or digesting the steps required. You might find you end up with the eggs beaten, flour added, but the cake is awful as you've omitted the sugar. Or you get to the end of building your chest of drawers only to find that the drawers don't fit because you've put the runners in upside down. Frustrating and time-wasting. If you'd taken the time to carefully read the instructions and ensure you understood them, you would have ultimately saved time and delivered a better result. Now consider the time you take to conduct relationship-building conversations with your colleagues at the beginning of and during your collaboration as the equivalent of reading and processing the instructions, except in this case, you and your colleagues are co-creating the instructions that will ensure your collaborative relationship works well.

The approach I take is one I've developed from my training and work as an executive coach, coach supervisor and facilitator over many years. It's based around creating a psychological 'contract' and is particularly valuable in establishing psychological safety in your relationship, by which I mean the foundation for building open, resilient and trusting relationships – the basis for effective collaboration.

Useful in any situation where collaboration is required, this approach focuses on making the implicit, those things we don't often think or talk about, explicit. Specifically, it creates clarity around needs and expectations and agreement about how these will be met. It's based around the acronym AIME©,[7] which stands for:

A – Agree jointly shared, measurable outcomes

I – Iron out assumptions

M – Make needs and expectations explicit

E – Evaluate and review repeatedly

AIME also provides a framework which makes it easier to address a situation when things go awry. Feelings emerge as people work together, and the structured conversations allow these feelings to be explored while the agreed ways of working are used as a frame of reference for how to

---

7   Copyright M Gregory 09/22

address them. When a co-facilitator and I experienced a breakdown in how we were working together, using this model allowed us to express our feelings, recognise which expectations or needs were not being met and get ourselves back on track. This led to us working more cohesively, benefiting not only us, but also our client.

Using the AIME approach helped me when working with a client recently. Sasha was the MD of a business going through a major transition. Following a merger, her leadership team had new members and their remit was now larger and more complex. Two of the new members were temporary as a new director who would be their manager was still being recruited.

Sasha reached out to me because, although the team was coping with a much bigger workload and agenda, she was concerned about the sustainability of this, and little time had been given to the team getting to know each other or understanding each other's roles. This resulted in duplication of effort, reduced efficiency and confused messages to the wider business.

HOW AN "AIME" APPROACH ENABLED COLLABORATION

1. Agree on shared, measurable outcomes

Before embarking on the project, Sasha and I met to set the work up for success. I asked

Sasha what success would look like for her and the team. She stated that she wanted the team to know and understand each other better, and for there to be an increased sense of cohesion and more clearly understood ways of working that would reduce duplication and confusion.

I also asked what evidence would demonstrate this had been achieved. She quickly identified dealing directly with each other as the need arose rather than scheduling time, a better use of meeting time and an increased focus on strategy and its implementation.

2. Iron out assumptions

Asking Sasha the assumptions she might have about our work together brought to light the need to create clarity around timescales and how she would communicate the purpose of the day to her team. This included ensuring they were available for preparatory one-to-one conversations with me.

To avoid any surprises, I explained that I might identify themes during my one-to-ones that would highlight issues she might not be aware of or comfortable with and that I would want to discuss this with her to agree the best way to address these during the workshop. I was glad I did so as some interesting dynamics subsequently arose, which we addressed in one of our review meetings.

3. Make needs and expectations explicit

I asked Sasha what specific needs or expectations she had of me and the process we were in. She recognised that the scale of change and the fact that a new director was still to join the team meant this was the start of their development journey and she would not be expecting everything to be resolved in one day. We agreed what realistically could be achieved and identified what follow-up in the short to medium term would be most likely.

Sasha also asked that I share any insights I had on the overall dynamics of the team, with a view to supporting her leadership. As a coach, I have a strong need to create psychological safety for everyone involved in any of the work I embark on. We agreed that to support this, Sasha would let her team know she was open to their feedback and that conversations held during the day would remain confidential between them and be treated constructively, without retribution.

4. Evaluate and review repeatedly

On a regular basis I checked in with Sasha about the themes that were emerging from the diagnostics, and my design suggestions for the day. We checked that her needs and expectations were being met and vice versa. Using AIME as a structured conversation for building our relationship, we established open and honest communication, ensuring the work and our relationship stayed on track and sustaining our collaborative approach.

Addressing concerns became a natural, constructive part of how we communicated. For example, during the diagnostics a theme of conflict in the team emerged which was draining team energy and holding them back. I thought it was important to explore this in the workshop, but I wasn't sure how Sasha would feel about this. Having got into the rhythm of being open and clear with each other, this conversation was straightforward and we agreed on an approach we were both happy to take.

Summary

A collaborative approach is an empowering way to work together, to navigate change and emerging situations. It takes self-awareness and a willingness to be open to other people's agendas and needs. To establish successful collaborative relationships, remember to slow down to speed up and use AIME as a structure for conducting the supportive conversations that will keep your work together on track.

Mary Gregory is a leadership consultant, coach and author of the bestselling book *Ego – Get Over Yourself and Lead*. She helps leaders navigate change, deal with adversity, strengthen confidence and resilience and create a career or business they love.

Mary works in person and online, facilitating both one-to-one and lively interactive group sessions. She empowers her clients to access personal resources through a range of insightful tools and models so they can confidently take positive action. She draws on learning and experience gained as a therapist in child psychiatry and through leading change across companies such as Ralph Lauren and Tesco. With an MSc in change management, she is a qualified coach and coach supervisor.

🌐 www.marygregory.com

in www.linkedin.com/in/marygregory

CHAPTER 6

When Collaboration Fails

LISA WEBB

When I first sat down to plan this chapter, I wasn't aware of how much collaboration I did. The more I thought about it, the more apparent it became that collaboration is an integral part of everything I do. After all, I'm a designer – I design branding and marketing pieces for other people's companies. If I didn't collaborate with my clients, I wouldn't be able to understand their needs well enough to produce meaningful work for them.

Collaboration, due to its nature of mixing different views and personalities, is not always straightforward or successful. Part of the crux of successful collaboration is being able to identify the differing strengths and weaknesses of the collaborators. Even then things can go wrong and unsuccessful collaborations can be costly in many ways. Not only can a bad experience have financial implications, it can also knock your confidence and make you wary of embarking on future collaborations which might have a different outcome.

A collaboration went wrong for me in 2008 when my business partner and long-time collaborator decided to disappear along with all the money in our account. Coincidence? I doubt it. Overnight I lost not only someone I thought of as a close friend and colleague, but also our hard-earned profits. I was devastated by the apparent betrayal but I was also embarrassed by what I considered my own stupidity – how could I have let this happen? There were moments when I wasn't sure how my business could continue, or even if I wanted it to.

After much soul-searching, I came to the realisation that it wasn't actually stupidity but rather naivety which had led me to the position I was in. I was so focused on bringing in work and maintaining a high level of creative output that I had lost touch with the running of my business. I had given my business partner so much power that I couldn't even log into my own accounts. At the time, I hadn't thought this was a problem; after all, we had different strengths. Business was good and I believed we worked well together.

Suffice to say I blamed myself for a long time and although I know now that what happened was not my fault, I must acknowledge that I did not make sure I had any safeguards in place to prevent it. I learnt from my mistakes and implemented that knowledge going forward. Not only do I now maintain creative control over the contracts I accept, I also keep a firm grip on the administrative side of things. The key thing to remember is that when collaborations don't work or when they don't go in the direction you had hoped for, there are almost always opportunities to learn and to grow – I just don't recommend you make them as extreme as mine.

Lessons learnt when collaboration goes wrong

After the incident, I was understandably wary of collaboration for quite some time, but my business suffered without it. It was only when I made peace with what had happened, stopped blaming myself for what I perceived to be a failure on my part, and allowed myself to start trusting others again, albeit with a higher level of personal protection, that my business started to boom again. Reopening the door to collaboration allowed a new wave of projects and professional relationships to blossom.

Nowadays, I'm acutely aware of the benefits of collaborative working and it is a fundamental part of my business. I no longer work solely as an anonymous behind-the-scenes designer for large conglomerates; I have redesigned my business in such a way that I can collaborate directly with my clients to produce the best possible results for them. I collaborate with other designers, marketing departments, other entrepreneurs and, perhaps most significantly, my clients.

Collaborating has improved both the creative and the business side of my company. It has given me a sounding board for new ideas and concepts and has broadened my business horizons. It has forced me to look up and out and not always be so focused on the minutiae of the working day (which is easily done when you're a solopreneur). My creativity has always benefited from collaboration and often in ways that surprise me. For example, collaboration has in the past helped me reframe my initial approach to a problem, which in turn enabled unexpected solutions to present themselves. That's the thing about two heads: often they really are, as the proverb goes, better than one. Successful branding for any client is always a collaborative effort. It's no secret that the more each party puts in, the more successful the outcomes tend to be.

I'm passionate about producing strong branding for individuals and small businesses so that they can attract the right kind of clients to maximise their business. Many of the people I work with are not creatives themselves and so it's particularly important for us to trust each other. I trust them to tell me who they are and explain what they do. They trust me to hear them and to embody that in their branding.

As well as collaborating with clients from different industries, I often collaborate with other designers. As I mentioned earlier, this kind of collaboration has enabled me to explore different approaches to solving problems. It has exposed me to new trends, new ways of working and even new software. It has also made me braver. It takes the pressure off and allows ideas to flow more freely. Ultimately, it's a fulfilling way to work that not only helps with meeting deadlines but also delivers on creativity.

One of the most rewarding collaborations I've been involved with started at the beginning of the first UK lockdown in 2020. Many small businesses were in turmoil, my own included. An air of panic set in and projects were put on hold as companies reassessed their needs. With no end to the pandemic in sight, it was hard to see how some of us would survive.

I was approached by Hela, one of the founders of Sister Snog, a networking club I belonged to. Pre-Covid, Sister Snog had been lively in-person and event-based networking. Suddenly, this was no longer a possibility. Hela invited me to be part of the team she was creating to help her migrate Sister Snog to running online. I didn't think twice and jumped at the chance, even though it seemed daunting. Repositioning an existing brand is always an exciting endeavour and in this case the brainstorming and planning sessions with four other female business owners was cathartic. It was great to be involved in a team where everyone had distinct roles to fill, and I wanted it to work. I wanted to continue attending but, unless we found a way to make the business viable in a newly pandemic-ridden world, it wouldn't survive. It was like losing your favourite shop on the high street and wishing you'd supported it more when it was there.

The mutual support from these women at such a strange time in our lives was precious, with all of us working towards a common goal. The whole experience made me realise that good professional relationships are even more vital when the world takes unexpected turns outside of our control. It was an absolute joy to work in a team of amazing businesswomen and it cemented our existing relationships, which can only bode well for all our futures.

Summary

There is no one-size-fits-all formula for successful collaboration, but there are things we can do to give ourselves the best possible chance.

TIPS FOR COLLABORATION

1. Start with honest communication

I decided a long time ago that all branding commissions should begin with an honest conversation; it's important to know you're on the same page and that you can work well together. The same is true for every collaboration, whether it's with other creatives or with a client. By creating rapport in this way, I ensure a comfortable and relaxed environment where meaningful interactions flow naturally. It's not that you can't do a great job for someone if you don't get along, it's just that it's much more rewarding for both parties when you do.

2. Develop your USP

Once a job is commissioned, we hold a discovery session with the aim of finding out what has led the client to the point they're at and establishing the direction they want their journey to take. We delve deeper into their vision. By pinpointing what drives the client in their business pursuit, who they want to help and what the point of their work is (over and above making a profit), we begin to understand their brand positioning possibilities, target markets and ideal clients. In other words, we start to develop their USP, or as I like to call it, their YouSP. All of this work is done before any design work is even thought about.

3. Build positive relationships

Collaboration continues beyond this point throughout the design process. It's important to keep your clients in the loop and make them feel a part of the process. That's how you get them to trust and believe in you but it's also a way of measuring your own design progress. When I asked Karen Skidmore, a recent client of mine, what she enjoyed about

our one-to-one branding workshop, she said
that she valued my commitment to finding a
way forward, that she felt I loved what she did
and was 100% invested in the project. Positive
relationships are also at the heart of repeat
business and there's no harm in preparing for
the future while delivering in the present.

4. Set clear expectations

It's important to understand what's expected
of you and of the other party/parties involved
so you can trust each other to do what you
need to do. Be honest about what you want
to achieve. Play to your strengths and let
your collaborators play to theirs. I have found
that most conflict comes from people not
understanding what their role is. Put things
in writing so you know where you stand, and
be clear about deliverables − both personally
and together as a whole. Ensure everyone
understands the timeframes; nothing ruins a
good collaboration like missing the deadline.
Trust your gut, trust the process and trust each

Lisa Webb is a designer who's passionate about helping women aged forty and beyond with their branding so they attract the right clients to their business. After working in several design agencies throughout her twenties, the opportunity to start Pinkfrog Design presented itself in 2000 and she has never looked back. Pinkfrog is a boutique agency based in sunny South London, which has seen numerous highs and lows; it's been far from plain sailing but each wave has made the company more resilient.

Lisa's clients range from solopreneurs to companies listed on the stock exchange. She is fascinated by people's stories, how luck or love or adversity brought them to this moment and where they can go from there; being part of their business journey is a pleasure. She's also a lover of football and rainbows, and she's partial to a cuppa.

🌐 www.pink-frog.co.uk

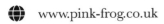 www.instagram.com/pinkfrogdesign

PART 3

Using collaboration to develop and grow your business

CHAPTER 7

Levels Of Collaboration

TRACEY BARR

Collaboration means different things to different people. To me, it's the secret ingredient in successfully working for yourself. It's a mindset, a way of working with others where you draw on each person's skills, knowledge, expertise and resources to help everyone achieve their goals. When you set up your own business, you have a choice. You can go it alone and try to do everything by yourself, or you can share your journey and work with others to get to where you want to be quicker and better.

There are many different levels of collaboration, ranging from informal business networks to more formal partnerships. Each serves a particular purpose, and which option is right for you will depend on the maturity of your business and what you're looking to get from the collaboration.

Level 1: Business networks

- These are often the first port of call for business owners looking to raise the profile of their company and build their contacts. Informal and with a light-touch approach, they bring entrepreneurs together virtually and/or in-person, encourage them to connect and help them generate business from one another.

- The most effective forums connect people who own or work in businesses in a local area. They not only help you to promote and grow your business but, through regular local meetups and events, they also provide you with that sense of belonging you may be missing working as a solopreneur.

Level 2: Membership clubs

- Membership clubs are the perfect place to meet fellow entrepreneurs and build long-term, trusted relationships with people who share a similar mindset and values to you. They are a hotbed for making new connections, learning and sharing knowledge, and for generating and exchanging creative ideas, which often lead to exciting new ventures; and they provide expert advice and support.

- There are lots to choose from and they can be expensive, so make sure to do your research. Take your time to decide which is the right fit for you and best meets your needs. Once you've joined, find the time to engage with others and be an active member so that you make the most of the benefits on offer.

Level 3: Professional networks

- If you're looking to extend your reach to new clients, sectors or geographies, or to build your experience and credibility, joining a professional network in your field is a great place to start. Some act as an intermediary, bringing together independent consultants and small businesses to create virtual teams with the right mix of skills and experience to successfully collaborate on bidding for and delivering client projects.

- Getting into these networks isn't easy. The application process is rigorous and selection criteria are tough. Even once you've been accepted, you need to invest time to keep at the top of people's minds – but the effort is worth it.

Level 4: Alliances and partnerships

- If you're looking to collaborate to set up a new venture, develop a new service or work with another business to jointly bid on a new contract, you need to put formal arrangements in place to build an alliance or partnership.

- In my field of independent consulting, the associate model is an excellent way to collaborate with niche consultancy firms. Often used by small firms looking to work regularly with a small base of independents with rich expertise in their field, it creates a win-win situation for both parties by providing the consultancy firms with an agile, experienced workforce they can draw on as and when they need to at a variable cost, and the consultants with a steady stream of project opportunities they would not have access to through their own networks.

Where to find collaborative partnerships

My business, The Strategic Link, is a niche consultancy firm that provides independent strategy advice, primarily to healthcare organisations, investors and policy makers. I set it up in 2004, building on the rich experience I'd gained and the connections and relationships I'd built from over twenty years of working in leadership and senior roles in strategy consulting, healthcare and small and medium-sized enterprises.

Today, the majority of my clients come to me directly through word of mouth or personal recommendation. Many are repeat clients who I've worked with before – but this hasn't always been the case. In the early years, while I was building my profile and establishing myself as an independent consultant, I struggled to generate a steady stream of high-quality consultancy projects. Despite having a well-established personal network, I would often find myself with a dry spell between projects with no income coming in, sometimes for several weeks. I knew I needed to come up with ways to collaborate to extend my reach beyond my own connections.

I researched the marketplace and came across a number of new virtual consultancy models developed by ex-management consultants and built around professional networks that effectively match experienced independent professionals to potential project opportunities, in line with their knowledge and skills. The particular appeal of these models to me is that I remain free to choose the type of clients I work with and the projects I work on as well as when and how much of my time I work through them. Another plus, which many of you might relate to, is I don't have to bill and chase the client for payment, so the financial risks are lower and the invoices are paid quicker than when I work direct. This does come at quite a high cost as it is the consultancy firm, not me, who owns the client relationship.

The first network I applied to was Eden McCallum, an early mover and now an established leader in this space. Over the first five years of my business, almost 40% of my work came from projects I became involved with through them. These projects were interesting and challenging, with clients from outside my own network. The fee rates were attractive, and I got to lead a team of fellow independents all at different stages of their careers – something I missed from my corporate days.

Many years later, I'm still part of the talent pool at Eden McCallum. I'm also on three other similar professional networks – Odgers Connect, Co-Match and A-Connect. Each provides me with a steady flow of exciting opportunities both in the UK and overseas. Although today the majority of my work comes to me directly, these networks remain an important route to market for me – never more so than during the pandemic – and each year I get to work with one or two new clients via this path. I invest time and effort in maintaining my relationships with the networks and in being an active commentator on LinkedIn to ensure I remain at the forefront of people's minds so that when the right opportunity arises, they think of me.

Although there have been tough times – the pandemic was definitely a challenge – I haven't looked back. I love what I do and remain as enthusiastic and passionate as I was when I started all those years ago. I'm incredibly proud of the business I've built, the clients I've worked with, the projects I've worked on. I've learnt a lot of lessons along the way, especially about not trying to do everything myself and how, when and who to collaborate with as I look to develop and grow my business.

Summary

Collaboration can help you in a multitude of ways. While you might find it hard to let go initially, the more you collaborate, the better you will understand how working with others can help your own business flourish and the better you will get at doing it. Collaboration isn't a science, it's an art. There are no hard and fast rules for how to effectively use collaboration to grow your business; it's a learning curve and each person's experience is unique. That said, I do have a few top tips, drawn from my own experience.

TIPS FOR COLLABORATION

1. Build your network

Trust is the foundation to successful collaboration. It's important to find the right places to meet like-minded people who can support and encourage you in developing your business. Once you've found them, create space in your diary and invest time in building relationships to help you understand their business, their background, their skills and experience and, most importantly, their values and what makes them tick. I have found those people in professional networks for independent consultants, in membership clubs for female business owners, and among the alumni from the companies I worked with before going it alone.

2. Know your 'why'

Be clear about why you are looking to collaborate and how it will help you to achieve your ambitions and the goals you have set for yourself and your business. That way, you can target the people or businesses you want to work with. When you're approached with a proposition to partner, it can be tempting to rush in and say 'yes' straightaway. Count to ten. Take time to carefully consider whether it's the right path for your business and the best investment of your time or your funds. Remember, it's OK to say no.

3. Choose the right partner

A key ingredient to successful collaboration is working with the right partner, but how do we choose? Yes, they need to have the complementary skills, knowledge or relationships you need – be that to build a new business, develop a new service or

win a new client – but it's more important
to find someone you trust, someone who's
open, honest, shares your values and is as
passionate and committed as you are. It
should also be someone you enjoy spending
time with and who, when the going gets
tough, will be there to pick you up and put a
smile back on your face.

4. Make sure you're on the same page from the get-go

Spend time writing a clear brief that sets
out what you are looking to achieve; what
your shared goals and expectations are;
what success will look like and how you'll
measure it; what your respective roles and
responsibilities are. Without this, you risk being
on different paths.

A common cause of friction comes from
avoiding an upfront conversation about
money. It's something we are often
uncomfortable talking about, but if you don't
clearly establish the financial terms and are
not transparent about how any income, costs
and financial risks will be shared, you risk a
problem arising further down the line. Sadly,
too many business relationships break down as
a result of this.

5. Just do it

Many of us women who set up our own businesses have an independent mindset; we're happy and used to doing everything for ourselves and don't want to rely on others. While being independent has its merits, it can hold us back from growing our businesses as the opportunities for personal growth, development and innovation and for sharing skills, knowledge, experience and expertise – part and parcel of working for a corporate – are only there if you invest the time to collaborate with others to create them.

Tracey Barr is a highly regarded independent strategy consultant specialising in healthcare. She combines thirty-five years' experience with analytical, consulting and relationship management skills to help her clients develop, grow, improve and successfully exit their businesses.

In 2020 she was selected as an *f:*Entrepreneur #ialso 100, a campaign showcasing inspiring female business leaders as role models for small business owners. She loves to share her knowledge and insights on LinkedIn, so reach out and connect.

⊕ www.thestrategiclink.co.uk

in www.linkedin.com/in/tracey-barr-healthcare-strategy-digital

CHAPTER 8

Achieve Success Through Collaboration

HENRIETTE DANEL

Collaborations between independent entrepreneurs are increasingly popular across every area of business. Naturally, people who work together and share expertise with others in their field benefit from these relationships. In the past, a sense of competition between business owners has stymied collaboration: the fear was that working with 'the competition' meant risking your best-kept business secrets being revealed to your competitors. That fear is giving way to the increasingly popular idea that every business has its own unique value, and that collaborating allows us to learn from each other rather than just compete.

If we spend too much time comparing our business to others – which social media certainly encourages – it's difficult not to feel awed by others' achievements but all too easy to take an overly critical view of our own, even if we are just launching and those around us are well established. These thoughts and feelings can be so insidious that we barely notice our own negative self-talk. At these times, fear of competition is high and collaboration feels like a fantasy.

When faced with self-doubt, it might feel counterintuitive to reach out to the competition, but collaborating with others can help you appreciate your uniqueness and the skills and experience you bring to the table. You might start to appreciate what you have to offer that no one else has – even your business hero; when you begin to collaborate and communicate, you might be surprised (and a bit relieved) to find out your heroes have moments of self-doubt too. Sharing these common fears and worries could help to alleviate them for everyone.

By collaborating, you will come to appreciate how special you and your business are. Just as you have a unique way of thinking, being and moving through the world, your business is also unique – because it's yours. The sooner you realise this, the sooner you will stop comparing and competing, and start collaborating – with all the opportunities that brings. Greatness and success come through working with others; collaboration is key to achieving your goals and dreams.

Collaboration can offer you:

- **A change of perspective:** When you step outside your comfort zone, you discover more about yourself. You might be surprised to learn what you're capable of and to discover the skills and strengths you possess.

- **A world of possibilities:** Collaborating often leads to more opportunities to collaborate. Just being in the room with other businesspeople will open possibilities for further work.

- **A chance to be inspired:** It can be wonderful to share space, time and energy with inspiring individuals. When collaboration works well, you'll go away feeling positive, re-energised and ready to face the next challenge.

- **Financial gain:** Business owners often collaborate with the common goal of increasing sales.

- **Better resources:** Collaborating might give you access to resources – facilities, staff, equipment – of a size or quality you currently couldn't afford alone.

- **Intellectual benefit:** You will learn from each other's expertise, knowledge and capabilities.

- **The human touch:** Relationships with and support from peers in your field are priceless.

Collaborating with your competition

Steaming cup of tea in hand, I gazed out of my kitchen window into my garden. It was early December 2019; the winter sun rose late in the morning, and this morning was to be a special one. There wasn't a cloud in the sky and the rays of sunrise were filtering through the trees, creating a beautiful red-and-orange hue over the garden. I was slowly sipping my tea, mesmerised by the beauty of the view, and savouring the moment. It was a moment of clarity, stillness and magic – and it was then, in the peace of that morning, that the idea hit me that changed everything for me and my business.

Full of excitement, I ran up the stairs to my office and frantically scribbled all my thoughts and questions into my notebook and then, when I was done, I sat and slowly read back through what had just poured out of me onto the pages. When I had finished reading, I sat back. This is crazy, I thought. It will never work. Who would want to do this collaboration with me?

Still, something about the idea spoke to me and, despite my doubts, I started reaching out to a few businesswomen I knew – ten in total. To my amazement, all ten of them came back to me and excitedly said yes to my proposal. Oh dear. Now this was real, and I would have to see it through!

On 18 December 2019, I created The Entrepreneurial Success Giveaway. The idea was to recruit between thirty and forty female entrepreneurs from all over the world to take part. The project's aim was to grow the email lists of all the collaborators by adding valuable new leads and contacts to their address books. Each collaborator provided their lead magnet for The Giveaway, and the only marketing they needed to do was to share the project with their audiences. If each collaborator did this, with all of our audiences combined, we would have enough traffic coming to us for The Giveaway to work.

I wanted to make sure that our audience would get high-quality content from the other collaborators to help them in their businesses, and to make The Giveaway attractive for them. For this reason, I was selective about who I worked with and made sure that the lead magnets were of real value. The Giveaway was to be a one-stop shop for individuals to get everything they needed for their business. Instead of surfing the internet for hours, they could simply get content of value and interest to them by clicking on The Giveaway.

For the whole of that December and January, I interviewed potential collaborators and built The Entrepreneurial Success Giveaway from scratch. Then, on 24 February 2020, we launched The Giveaway for the first time. It was a huge success and many collaborators asked if we would do it again, so we agreed. We launched again in May, and then again in November. By our final launch, over 1000 people attended over a five-day period and every single one of my collaborators walked away with between 100 and 300 leads from those five days alone.

The Entrepreneurial Success Giveaway was a success to a degree I'd never expected and in ways that surprised and delighted me. It taught me a huge amount about collaboration and how to get it right. My business excelled, my confidence soared and I became known as 'the lady who arranged The Giveaway collaborations' – a title I could be proud of.

In addition to learning how to create international collaborations, I learnt something even more valuable from The Giveaway: if you get the spark of some magical idea, you must execute it. This idea is the doorway to a journey that will change everything for you. No matter how scary, inconceivable or unreal it might seem, you need to listen to your gut and follow your heart. Don't worry about all the details of how you're going to do it, just commit and go for it.

Summary

In my years as a business owner, I've noticed how difficult it is to find existing collaborative projects that are completely aligned with your values and needs – and even if you do, you'll have to pitch to get your foot in the door with them. Why not initiate your own? Put yourself in the driver's seat and you can work with the people you want, the way you want, on the goals that are important to you. It is entirely possible – and enjoyable – to run your own collaborative project. Will Smith once said, 'You just decide what it's gonna be, who you're gonna be, you just decide. And then from that point the universe is going to get out your way.'[8] Often, we get so hung up on working out the how that we never start. Take a leap of faith, commit to the seemingly impossible and begin – everything will become clear along the way, trust me.

TIPS FOR COLLABORATION

1. The end goal

Before you ask your collaborators in, it's key to know what your main goal is for your project. This will affect everything, from who you invite to how you manage communication. Having a clear agenda allows everyone involved to pull in the same direction from the beginning; the last thing you want is one person trying to build audience relationships while another is increasing leads. Whether your aim is to raise everyone's sales, cross-promote one other or enhance visibility, everyone must be clear about what the goal of the project is.

---

8   J Miller, 'Will Smith's Philosophy', Medium (24 March 2013), https://medium.com/@jonnym1ller/will-smiths-philosophy-668f37dd51b1, accessed 30 November 2022

2. Contact

Write a list of all your contacts within your field or industry, then add to that all of the people you know from other fields who have similar audiences to you. Select who you'd like to work with, choosing double the number of collaborators you'll actually need as not everyone you ask will say yes. Reach out to each person/company, inviting them to an introductory conversation about your project. Have an actual conversation rather than directing them to a sales page – it's more personal, and you'll get a better sense of their commitment and interest.

3. Selection

When it comes to selecting who will make the final cut for your project, choose wisely and keep these three musts in mind:

- Your collaborators must bring different but complementary skill sets.

- They must all share your energy and excitement for the project.

- Everyone must share a mindset around how to approach the project and an understanding of its goals.

4. Clarity

Make sure communication is crystal clear and set out your terms from the start. Everyone needs to know exactly what is expected of them and by when – you don't want one or two people doing all the heavy lifting while everyone else is twiddling their thumbs. It's essential that you have written contracts between yourself and your collaborators from the beginning to avoid misunderstandings, and to ensure that all financial agreements are legal, protected and understood by everyone.

5. Commitment

The most important step in any project is to make sure that everyone involved is fully committed to it, and to what you all want to achieve together.

Henriette Danel is a business coach working with female entrepreneurs and business owners in the service-based industry to help them continuously attract more clients. She's also the host of The Entrepreneurial Success Podcast and a public speaker.

Henriette's speciality lies in her unique ability to take something complicated, dissect it and put it back together in a way that's easy to understand and implement – a skill which helps her clients gain clarity and achieve amazing results in record time.

Henriette believes that running a business should be fun, encouraging and done with integrity. It requires your commitment and clarity. Once you're focused, signing up a continuous succession of clients happens naturally.

🌐 www.henriettedanel.com

in www.linkedin.com/in/henriettedanel

📷 www.instagram.com/henriette.danel

CHAPTER 9

Climbing Mountains Together

VICTORIA BURT

Collaboration is giving and taking, sharing expertise and experience, planning and developing. It's horizon-broadening and relationship-building. It's 'I've got a brilliant idea...' and 'It could be even better if...' It's something that is greater than the sum of its parts. Much greater. It's feeling like you have climbed to the top of the mountain on your own, then walking with another person to one that is even higher and has an even better view.

When people ask if I am interested in collaborating, it makes my heart sing. What? You really want to work with me? It is an affirmation of what you are doing, confirmation that you are getting things right and that other people want to align themselves with your ideas, business and brand. It's a huge compliment and something that should be celebrated and championed. In the same way, when you ask someone to collaborate with you, you are saying, 'I trust you, I value your expertise and I want to work with you.' Don't underestimate what such an accolade can do for a person's confidence or the positive effect that it can have on them and, in turn, their business.

My business has only been up and running for four years. For the first eighteen months, I was developing my brand while working part-time at a primary school. If I'm honest, I had no idea how much was involved in running your own business. The admin, marketing, branding, customer service, strategy, planning, cups of tea (turns out I'm fuelled by tea) – it's all down to you.

As a business grows, other people might be brought in to do various jobs, but at the beginning you are usually on your own. There is no one on the desk next to you (or, as it used to be in my case, in the classroom next door) to ask for clarification of something, advice or validation of an idea. I learnt that when you are in charge of your own enterprise and navigating your way through the world of small business, surrounding yourself with a group of like-minded people is key.

Building your start-up business through collaboration

I am lucky enough to have been introduced to a number of businesswomen's groups where members support, encourage and champion one another. I have met many amazing people who are heading up their own businesses and projects. All of them are willing to share advice and experience and I can honestly say that being part of these communities is one of the highlights of having my own company.

As a woman, the business groups that I am part of are communities for women. We have a different experience in business to men and we often start our businesses for different reasons. Being part of a group of women who can give you honest feedback, advice and suggestions is invaluable and has been a lynchpin in the development and growth not only of my business but also of me as a person. These groups are wonderful; they are life- and business-changing. I come out of every meeting feeling like I'm walking on air and ready to be as successful as I possibly can.

So far, I haven't found a similar group for both men and women, and therein lies my first story of collaboration. I have been the member of a small gym in my local town for around twelve years. It's a brilliant place and isn't a traditional type of gym, which is probably why I've been a member for so long.

The gym is owned by someone who used to work in a gym in the City and wanted to bring his expertise, knowledge and skills to a wider range of people in the town where he lived. A personal, bespoke service but not at City prices. I had wanted to run my own business for a while, and his talk of the triumphs and pitfalls of being a business owner interested me. Now that I have my own business, the conversations are less one-sided, and I have something to bring to the table.

I shared my experience of the business groups that I am a member of, and showed him the photos on social media of me going to swanky locations to network with amazing businesswomen, and he complained that there was nothing like that out there for men. This was something that I had noticed as well. At the time, this felt like a throwaway comment, in among the discussions of corporation tax, marketing, social media strategies etc.

Months (and the pandemic) went by, and he suggested we host a podcast together, discussing business ownership from the point of view of both men and women. We could chat between ourselves and invite along small business owners to discuss certain topics, to share expertise and perhaps talk about how the experiences of men and women in business differ, and how we can learn from and support one another.

I liked this idea: by collaborating in this way I would be able to create a podcast, something I feel I wouldn't have been able to do on my own. Our collaboration didn't end there; in fact, this was just the beginning. The podcast was put on hold while we thought about whether this could become something bigger. We chatted, discussed, planned and strategised. We mind-mapped, outlined, projected and took notes.

No longer just hosting a podcast (although that was still part of the plan), we were going to create a business group loosely based on the brilliance of the ones that I was a member of, but for both men *and* women. Through our discussions, we brought together our extensive ideas and experience and began to understand exactly what we wanted our club to look like and what we wanted it to achieve.

Not every idea is brilliant. At times suggestions are made and they are tweaked, expanded or simply thrown out altogether – this is part of the beauty of collaboration. You are working with someone. Our ideas are taking shape and, by early next year, we are hoping to launch. It feels exciting and certainly not something I could have achieved on my own, which is, in a nutshell, the essence of collaboration: you accomplish more. In our case, what started as one idea (the podcast) has developed by working together. Acorns become oaks and dreams become plans, and from a plan we achieve the goal.

The second collaboration, and something that is still in the discussion stage, is an idea in line with the business I already have: private tutoring. This came about as a result of meeting Kate, someone who has a similar business to me. We originally met through one of the women's business groups that I mentioned earlier, and now we regularly get together for coffee (normally courtesy of the John Lewis café) to talk business, share ideas, ask for advice and, in some way, be accountable to someone.

Meeting regularly, being in the same business, having similar career paths and of course getting on well, it is no surprise that a collaboration has come about, this time based on providing study resources for parents and children and extra support to children who need it, particularly in exams. By collaborating, we can spread the net across a wider area, reaching more families and gaining a bigger slice of the tutoring market.

We aim to create a whole package of products that is more than either of us offers at the moment. Time will have to be spent researching resources and what the offering will look like. As we are both busy, by collaborating we will be able to split the research, increasing the likelihood of our idea becoming a reality. As I said, the idea is in its infancy; there is lots more to talk about, more notes to be taken (I may have to buy another notebook) and our exact offering needs to be worked out. It is an exciting prospect, and in the meantime, it does mean that we will have to meet again for a few more of those John Lewis coffees!

Summary

You never know where collaboration may take you. Be open to ideas that come your way; they may not always be right for you, and you don't have to say yes to everything, but when you do get involved, you will realise the superpower of collaboration. I certainly didn't think I'd ever be a published author but, thanks to collaboration, here I am!

TIPS FOR COLLABORATION

1. Get out of the echo chamber

At times, collaboration works best when people are coming from different places and times in their lives, when they have different skills and experiences and work in different businesses altogether. Collaborations don't have to come about through people that are a similar age or from a similar background or business.

2. Don't take offence

When you are collaborating with someone, expect to have your suggestions talked through, expanded on, tweaked, changed and, on occasions, abandoned altogether. Collaboration means working together, so compromise may be needed. If you don't want anything that you bring to the collaboration table to be changed, make a reservation for one and talk to yourself.

3. Be brave and take the first step

I have often had an idea that's changed and changed and changed, sometimes to the point of being almost unrecognisable from the original concept. There is good reason for that. It is hard to know how something will work until it is put into practice, and at times you have to be brave and launch in. You can't wait until your big idea is perfect; it never will be, but don't be afraid to keep changing. This is equally true when it comes to collaboration: two brains might be better than one, but two brains also come with two opinions, so be prepared – you will quickly find that the first idea you had is just the beginning, not the finished article.

4. Jigsaw your skills

What do you have, what do you want? Collaboration is about sharing skills and expertise so that everyone gains. Not only are you creating something new, perhaps a service, product or concept, but you are increasing your brand worth and connections. Think about the type of person and business you want to align yourself with. What sort of people do you want to connect with? How will a collaboration elevate your business and brand identity?

Victoria Burt founded her company, Gilpin House Associates, in 2018. She has two businesses: a pop-up restaurant that she runs from her home with her husband, Peter, and a private tutoring company.

During the pandemic, the tutoring business had to pivot and went online. As a result, Vicky was able to hire more tutors; she now has a team of thirty-two tutors and the company is still growing.

In 2020 she was recognised as an *f:*Entrepreneur #ialso 100. This is a campaign that highlights inspiring female business leaders across the UK. This community showcases role models to support and inspire all small businesses.

🌐 www.additionstutoring.co.uk

f www.facebook.com/additionstutoring

f www.facebook.com/gilpinhousesupperclub

CHAPTER 10

The Secret Ingredient For Success

BONNY SNOWDON

Collaboration means working with others who share similar values but have different skills, thoughts and outlooks on life. It can seem uncomfortable, scary and as if someone else is taking your dreams and goals and dashing them against a wall. It takes strength and conviction to truly collaborate, particularly when it comes to business.

When I was considering what collaboration means, delegation came to mind and I got the two things mixed up. Having done quite a bit of thinking, now I know that they aren't the same at all – I'm not giving something to someone else to do in the way I want it done, I'm working with someone towards a shared goal. Usually, the people I choose to collaborate with have a totally different take on how to reach that goal.

Opening up to different thought processes is a great way to succeed in business. We all have our own patterns and our own, usually deep-seated, beliefs on how things should be done, and of course they are beneficial to our end goal, but often we get in our own way and can end up sabotaging things without even knowing it. Prior to starting my business, I had a vision in my head and I knew (or thought I knew) exactly what it looked like and how it was going to work. The thought of collaborating on something that I had been dreaming about for quite some time was unnerving.

Having similar values when collaborating with others is important, and something I strive for within my community. Two of my core values are faith (that things will always work out OK) and open-mindedness, and these were tested to quite an extent when it came to collaborating. Understanding the value of collaboration means you have to go through the discomfort and come out the other side – you can't have a true opinion about it unless you've experienced it, and it's well worth experiencing. Comfort zones are just that – comfortable. Outside of that zone is definitely uncomfortable, but can and will lead to exciting things, as I found out through being brave enough to collaborate with someone I didn't know but felt a deep connection with. I trusted my instincts and took that leap of faith.

Creating a membership model

Like many artists, I had a dream of creating a sustainable business that could give me a better quality of life. Unlike many artists, I didn't believe the phrase 'starving artist', and I did believe I could make a living from my art.

One of six children, brought up in the 70s and 80s on a farm and then in a beautiful 14th-century deanery, I had a blessed childhood and held the belief, handed down from my mother, that everything would turn out OK and that I could do and be whatever I wanted. That belief held fast when I fell into art in 2016, and then decided to quit my job to become a full-time artist at the beginning of 2017 – after only six months of drawing.

Fast-forward to 2019 and I began teaching, using a third-party platform, Patreon. Teaching was something I was interested in as I love people, and my career quickly grew until I was making five figures each month. Previously, I had not been able to pay my supermarket bill on quite a few occasions, so to have an art business making six figures yearly was amazing.

I soon became disillusioned with Patreon – I had no control over their scrolling feed, their customer service or their strange payment system – so I started to dream about and plan my own teaching platform. I knew I needed help. I had researched the different membership platforms out there and decided I wanted to use Kajabi, and I had already started to put a website of sorts together. I put an advert out into the ether and received a number of proposals back. They all said the same thing: 'Yup, I can create a membership off the back of what you already have and it will cost you X amount.'

One proposal stood out from all the others, although my first reaction was to be a bit bristly. A British consultant from France suggested that we look at my brand and do a digital discovery of the membership I wanted to create, and said that it would be a contract of at least four months to start with while we went through an onboarding process and rebranding exercise. I had created my own website and was proud of it, and to have someone come in and say they wanted to change my brand and redo the whole thing was a bit of a shock.

I'm good at getting over myself and, although this proposal was going to cost five times more than the others I'd received, it was incredibly in-depth and the consultant was suggesting setting up a membership from scratch. I bit the bullet and decided to go along with her, and Lucy Hutchings Hunt became a member of my team both on a consultancy level and as a collaborator to build my new business.

Working with Lucy meant I had to open my mind to a different way of working; I had to listen to an expert who had done this before, and although she shared my core values, there were quite a few times when I wasn't comfortable with what she was suggesting. We quickly came up with the name of my new business,

Bonny Snowdon Academy, and with that names for the membership, Ignite, and for my courses. This was easy to do together. Lucy has a way with words and she also knows the membership market well.

One thing I found hard to agree on was that my membership would launch a few times a year and be closed between the launches. I found this difficult to comprehend and I spent quite a lot of time procrastinating over and trying to work out how it would work. Eventually, I decided nothing ventured nothing gained and took that large leap of faith into the unknown.

The most incredible thing about collaborating with someone who was more experienced and had a different outlook on life was that she pushed me; she pushed me out of my comfort zone, she asked me questions that I had to dig deep to answer, and she introduced me to a new circle of inspiring people, to new ways of thinking and doing. By July, after five months of collaboration, we had come up with a plan.

I put my faith in Lucy. I'm someone who listens to their gut feeling and, although most of the things she was asking me to do didn't make sense at the time, I decided that it was better to be open-minded, that my belief in everything being OK was strong, and most of all that she had utter faith in me and my about-to-be-launched business. Lucy introduced me to a new way of marketing, to the world of funnels, pipelines, nurturing, email marketing and mailing lists. If I hadn't decided to collaborate rather than just let someone build a back-end membership, I would never have learnt all these things.

We launched on 17 September 2021 and welcomed in 700 members – an unbelievable amount of people, paying each month. Lucy collaborated with me; she helped me grow both the academy and as a person until we reached our first anniversary, when my business hit the 500K mark. If that isn't a great advertisement for collaboration, I don't know what is.

Summary

Don't be so rigid in your thinking that you struggle to accept help from others or to listen to different ideas. It might seem counterintuitive, but it's amazing what our minds will tell us when someone else suggests things that seem a little alien to us. I used to refuse to listen to podcasts where the guest had opposite views to me, but all this does is put us in our own little echo chamber. The world is a more vibrant place, and you're better positioned to make creative decisions, if you open yourself up to different thoughts and beliefs, which helps when collaborating.

TIPS FOR COLLABORATION

1. Be uncomfortable

I found that whenever Lucy asked me to do something I either hadn't heard about or felt differently about, instead of just saying 'No, I'm not comfortable with that', I would take the suggestion and put it out there – I would play around with it in my head, bring it up in my coaching sessions and try to be open-minded. Something I found incredibly useful was to ask myself why I was averse to the suggestion, why it was making me feel uncomfortable. This question would usually give me my answer, which enabled me to let go and make a decision from a place of having properly thought it through.

2. Listen to your gut

When you're trying to find someone to work and collaborate with, always listen to your gut. This should be something we do all the time anyway, but people often ignore a big gut reaction. First impressions can help, but are often incorrect. Have a few meetings and if your gut is telling you no, listen. To collaborate with someone, there has to be a positive connection, a sharing of values and a desire from both parties to get to the end goal.

Bonny Snowdon is Yorkshire born and bred, and works from her studio at home in a village with views over the Moors and the White Horse of Kilburn. Single mum to three relatively grown-up children, three large dogs, a new tiny puppy and a long-suffering cat, Bonny has built her business around her core values of faith that it will all be OK, community and kindness.

Having worked in corporates for nearly two decades, Bonny took up drawing in 2016 and quickly made her mark as a realism artist, artists' mentor and coach. She now runs a thriving business teaching people all over the world how to draw with coloured pencils.

🌐 www.bonnysnowdonacademy.com

❲f❳ www.facebook.com/bonnysnowdonacademy

📷 www.instagram.com/bonnysnowdonacademy

CHAPTER 11

Spot An Open Door And Walk Through It With A Smile

JADE THOMAS

Some people fear opening up their business to reveal the inner workings but, by seeking out collaborations, we can all evolve our services and offerings and find opportunities that we might not have considered before. We can bounce our wild ideas off each other and work out which ones might be worth developing.

An ever-growing web of connections and innovations comes from getting to know people. Investing your time in building connections with other entrepreneurs will reap rewards. Look beyond their job title and see the person behind the brand. You'll learn unique things about them, and you'll pick up tips and industry news which will give you a different perspective on your own business and may highlight new ways of thinking or processes that will elevate your services. Collaboration is exciting, so keep your eyes peeled for opportunities.

If you're busy running a small business, you can sometimes forget how to be a team player. Working as part of a collaborative group can help you all to achieve more, whether that's more sales, clients, efficiency, profits, exposure or acclaim. Trusting and being accountable to your team will fast-track you towards your shared goals. If things aren't going quite to plan, you can use your team for help and support.

Collaboration leads to innovation because of the unique approach, skills, expertise and understanding each person brings to the project. It is amazing to feel part of something innovative, and it's also a talking point, which in itself improves your ability to communicate clearly because all parties need clarity on the goals and desired outcomes of opening up to collaboration. If you can get your message across to your team of collaborators, you'll find it much easier when you need to explain it to your clients or potential clients.

I've always found that positivity breeds creativity and that a sprinkle of creativity makes all the good ideas materialise. Being open to the positive aspects of collaboration and support will have short-term and long-term benefits for everyone involved. A positive mindset also makes any opportunities for collaboration easier to spot, especially the ones that you may have thought were too epic or too huge for you to reach alone.

I'm not a fan of the 'fake it until you make it' motto, but I know that the act of putting a smile on your face shifts you into a more positive and confident mindset. Next time you have the chance to further your business with a collaborator, try popping a big old smile on your face and ask for a meeting to brainstorm mutual opportunities. The worst that could happen is they say no, but a 'Yes, definitely' is a more likely response. Go for it!

Opportunities to diversify through collaboration

I'm lucky enough to run two businesses and being open to collaboration has provided amazing opportunities in both of them. I launched my branding and website design business, Eau Rouge, in 2000 and I've collaborated with a range of different businesses over the decades. Sometimes I have been the driving force behind forming the dream team, and in other instances I have joined an existing collaboration. In branding projects, collaboration is fundamental to the success of implementing an identity. Having a lovely new logo and brand style is great, but when my clients have access to an aligned team that will create their on-brand photography, copywriting and printed elements, it brings their new product to life.

One of the most interesting collaborations I became part of was for a change management firm who needed a designer to make their ideas a reality. They were looking for a creative who could work with their clients' existing brand guidelines and create material that looked like it was generated in-house. For me, it was a brilliant opportunity to work as part of a team and to contribute to the brainstorming which helped make the final workbooks or team planners easy to understand and intuitive for employees to work through. It allowed me to design for much larger businesses than I would have approached by myself and it brought together many different perspectives from all the experts. We supported each other too, and the final outcomes were something we could all be proud of. Team work definitely does make the dream work.

My jewellery design business was born out of a thirst to design something tangible (and my love of sparkles!). I specialise in designing one-off pieces featuring rare gemstones, diamonds and precious metals. I made jewellery for friends when I was at school, but when I was nearing forty I decided to go back to college part-time to learn silversmithing. After completing my studies, I thought about how to bring jewellery into my career: I knew that the design was an aspect I loved, but felt that I didn't have enough hours in my diary to spend hand-making jewellery.

I wanted to collaborate with an experienced jewellery maker, and I took my time finding a company in Hatton Garden that I felt a lot of synergy with. We work well as a team and I trust that their skills and experience will lead to beautiful finished pieces. Because Hatton Garden is synonymous with diamonds, I've displayed some of my gem pieces in their prominent window to catch the eye of fellow colour-loving magpies.

There's something else you should know about me – I spend a lot of time at motor racing circuits as my husband has a passion for racing. It's exciting to watch his racing close up, but there is also a lot of time to kill between the races. I was sitting with some drivers and wives at a cold and wet circuit one day when an idea came to me about what was lacking on a race weekend – sparkle. There were race cars to admire, and a few well-thumbed glossy magazines scattered about in the driver's hospitality tent, but these were wealthy women with time on their hands and I spotted an opportunity.

When the dust settled from that race weekend, I contacted the race organisers and proposed a collaboration whereby I could set up a pop-up jewellery stand within their roving hospitality tent. It was a no-brainer for me: we struck up a commission-based deal, so no sales equalled no financial outlay. I love my pop-up jewellery shop weekends – the hospitality team have spent time getting to know my pieces and how I design, and it is a secure space in which to display hundreds of thousands of pounds' worth of my jewellery.

Trust is a huge part of choosing who to buy jewellery from, and having the backing of such a respected race series helped me to forge my reputation in the paddock and gave me confidence in my fledgling jewellery business. Now, whenever I host my shop, I get a stream of racing drivers discussing their upcoming big birthday or anniversary needs and they know I'm a good brainstormer for gifts, even if it isn't jewellery. Being there has led to branding and web design opportunities too.

Summary

Collaborating strategically leads to more of the work you love and with clients you might not have met working alone. Walk through that door with the right attitude and the opportunities for growth will shine brightly for you. I can't wait to spot my next collaboration opportunity – it fills me with excitement and I hope this book and the experiences of the women who have written it make you feel the same about what collaboration might do for you and your business.

TIPS FOR COLLABORATION

1. Visualise your ideal client

My best collaboration tip is to have a clear image of one or two of your ideal clients – not the businesses if you're B2B, but the actual people in the business. Take time to visualise these people to round out their personas. Give them names and ages, and work out details such as where they go on holiday, who they

spend their time with and what would make
their lives easier. The more you can pad out
your vision of these people, the better.

2. Think about how to meet their needs

When you know them inside out, you'll have
a clearer understanding of the problems and
issues they might face. By getting to 'know'
these ideal clients, you'll build a picture of
their values and personality. You'll understand
what they need to see, hear and feel to find
the meaning and inspiration in what you do.
If you take time to understand their brand
values and identify their pain points, you can
brainstorm ways to collaborate with other
businesses and seek out a strategic team of in-
tune collaborators, those who also understand
just what these clients need, and together
you can offer a streamlined, professional and
expert service to solve all the client's problems,
which feels right to them and makes you an
indispensable team.

3. Identify their core values

When I worked on the rebrand and
repositioning of a plant nursery, the new
owner and I dug deep into the essence of
what the business wanted to convey – how
it needed to feel to its ideal clients – and this
gave us the clarity to build the brand from its

core values of being connected, of the earth, and knowledgeable. Once we had this clarity, the brand was easy to design, but several other elements were needed to bring it to life, including signage, murals, photography and workwear. I have an address book full of connections, but I kept the ideal clients in mind when I chose the businesses to collaborate with on this specific project – they were all run by women I had met networking, and I felt confident that each of them would provide the level of service my client needed and stay true to the nursery's brand identity and values.

4. Celebrate each other's work

When the plant nursery project is complete, we can all showcase and promote each other's work, which is a fine way to grow and strengthen your network and professional relationships. When you work together, you get to highlight your own brand values and ways of working, and guess what: next time one of those ladies needs to collaborate with a branding designer who works strategically to unearth the unique essence of a brand, they'll call me.

Jade Thomas is the founder of two design businesses – one creates brands, the other designs jewellery. Both tell stories.

She finds the discovery fascinating: finding clients' values, ideal customers, and what makes them stand out. This leads to beautiful branding and websites that attract the right people and lasting business relationships. Brands that stand tall.

Similarly, with her gemstones – clarity is key. This refers to their quality and journey. Jade can tell you the date when most of them came out of the ground and show what they looked like before being cut and polished. They transform into stunning, unique pieces of precious jewellery.

Her clients love her work because it is unique and always matches their personalities.

 www.eaurouge.co.uk

 www.jadethomasjewellery.co.uk

CHAPTER 12

Meshing Together To Create Magic

ELENA BRENNAN

Collaboration is about forming a strong bond between like-minded small business owners, entrepreneurs or individuals who create magic together. When you mesh together on a collaborative project, you are in essence sharing your worlds. It can feel unnerving at first as you may be going outside your comfort zone, but forming a new relationship or nurturing an existing one to create an alliance is also rewarding. This joint effort can be short-term for one particular project, or it can be a long-term collaboration sustained over a period of time. The purpose is to reach an audience that is unfamiliar with you or your products, thereby helping to grow and expand your business into new arenas, increasing awareness and generating more sales.

Some collaborative efforts develop over time, sought out by you or presented to you as a natural progression in the next phase of your business. Others pop up after brainstorming an idea, or a meeting with someone new which evolves into an exciting and worthwhile proposition you can't resist exploring.

To grow your business, it's important to join forces with other companies or individuals who are on the same wavelength as you. As a female small business owner, I feel especially inclined to collaborate (wherever possible) with other female entrepreneurs. There's an inexplicable connection between us, a strong bond and a desire to team up, which you'll see illustrated in my chapter and the chapters written by my Sisters.

Collaboration can be multi-tiered or layered, much like a decadent Black Forest gateau. During the Covid pandemic, I stumbled across a UK-based exclusive membership club for female business owners called Sister Snog. Coincidentally, at the time I was planning to expand my online presence internationally. Being British (I was born in London and moved to America when I was twenty-six years old), it made sense to embark on this transition with a UK counterpart as a first step to bridging the gap.

Prior to Covid, all Sister Snog events were held in person but things quickly had to change to a virtual platform. Joining would only be worthwhile if I could make the most of the membership, which meeting virtually allowed me to do – so thank you to that thing called Covid that gave me the opportunity to re-establish my UK roots and begin to expand my audience internationally.

Since becoming a member, I have formed many collaborations, including hiring a fellow Sister as my UK shoe agent. I have also won Best International Business Woman of 2021, a prestigious UK accolade that recognises the achievement of women across a wide range of business categories in the UK and globally. This was the first time I had ever entered for a business award and it has paved the way for doing so in the future.

There's a common thread to our club, or perhaps it's better viewed as an equation: Sister Snog members + Connecting = Collaborating. This book would never have happened if fifteen like-minded female entrepreneurs hadn't connected through a shared desire to collaborate with other compatible female entrepreneurs. You just never know when the next collaboration is around the corner.

International collaborations

Collaboration has helped me to propel my business to the next level to a degree that I did not think was possible. I first opened my business in 2007, initially as a retail shoe boutique in Philadelphia with no online presence or national and international exposure. When I became a shoe designer in 2015, it was a dream come true and a natural progression to the next chapter. Designing shoes came from my desire to try something new and totally outside my comfort zone, but also something I was passionate about. With no experience in fashion design (my background was advertising and marketing), the best way for me to achieve this goal was to collaborate with a company that had the same ethos as me. After much thought, I decided to see if it was at all possible to partner with one of the shoe companies I had a long-term relationship with and, more importantly, one that I trusted and respected.

After I plucked up the courage, I contacted the US agent and distributor at ALL BLACK Footwear for ACL Footwear LLC based in Taiwan. We first met at a trade show I had attended just before I started my business and they were one of the first brands I carried in my boutique, so over eight years we had established a trustworthy relationship. When I initially asked if they would be interested in collaborating with me to produce my own shoe designs at their factory in Taipei, they explained that in the past they had only ever collaborated with large retailers, such as Anthropologie. At first they were hesitant, but the strong, passionate, trustworthy bond we had formed over the years must have helped to get the ball rolling. We sat down at the drawing board and discussed in minute detail how such a relationship would work. The most daunting task for me was to reach the high minimum quantities the factory required to put my designs into production. I was also concerned about whether my customers would like my work.

The process encouraged me to see things in a different light and to start designing my first shoe collection. All of a sudden, I was faced with learning a whole new set of techniques: the way shoes are designed, the various steps in the shoe production process, not to mention how to increase my budget to bring my ideas to fruition. Being forced to make business decisions in new territory was exciting but frightening.

The production cycle from start to finish was nine months, which may not seem like a long time but was long enough for me to learn the new skills that would elevate my business to the next level. It also allowed me time to prepare by hiring a PR firm and arranging the photo shoot so that I was ready to launch my brand: BUS STOP X. I formed new lifelong friendships with the owners and team at the factory (regardless of the language barrier), and I refer to the team in Taipei as my second family. The collaboration also helped me to gain national and international recognition.

My latest BUS STOP X endeavour is a collaborative three-piece accessories line created in tandem with a Montreal-based, woman-owned brand: HOTELMOTEL. Our two harmonious brands connected through Instagram, and after an initial face-to-face meeting in Philadelphia, the collection was designed over various Zoom calls. Each piece is handmade in Montreal by two passionate female artisans, Jessup and Bourget, and sold exclusively in Philadelphia.

There's another collaboration in the pipeline – a sock design with the fabulous Hela Wozniak-Kay, the owner and founder of Sister Snog – and I know there are many more collaborations to come, so I'm looking forward to seeing what's on the horizon.

Summary

As a small business owner, I tend to work independently and within my own silo. Even though we are a team of five incredibly talented women, I have chosen to make a lot of the major financial decisions on my own. I know I am not alone in this decision; many other small business owners have confessed to me that they struggle with this too.

This independent mindset can hold you back. As a leader, as well as understanding the day-to-day running of your business, it is of the utmost importance to implement strategies for your company to achieve long-term goals. Part of these plans should be to venture into even more collaborations. The key to creativity and progress in business is to collaborate as much as possible. It's inspiring and uplifting, and keeps your business feeling fresh and alive.

The essence of collaboration is to not be afraid, to follow your heart and to seek out opportunities. The benefits far outweigh any feelings of trepidation or intimidation. Be bold, be fearless and collaborate.

TIPS FOR COLLABORATION

1. Remember the three key considerations

When collaborating with another business or individual, there are three key things to take into consideration. There has to be a unified trust; I don't know how you can even consider venturing into a new business partnership without it. There needs to be harmonious enthusiasm from both parties; and lastly, of course, you need passion. Without passion, nothing is possible.

2. Communicate clearly

At every stage of the process, it's important to implement clear communication. It is difficult to collaborate if you're not organised, so make sure you have a system in place for achieving this. I recommend that you conduct regular status meetings. After each meeting, it is crucial that you issue notes with a clear call to action for each task. I know this sounds simple, but leaving things up in the air allows too much room for confusion and will delay the process, and it is essential to have everything in writing. No verbal agreements please.

3. Be careful who you choose

Without a doubt, my best collaboration tip is be careful who you collaborate with. Follow your gut instincts and do your research, making sure that it's a good fit and, most importantly, that the end goal is apparent to everyone. Both parties need to be on the same wavelength. By that, I mean there has to be some aspects of similitude for it to be a smooth and successful partnership. In the end, it's all about a strong relationship, sharing the same values and being on the same page. There's a lot at stake both financially and with respect to your reputation. Deciding to join forces with someone who can damage your good reputation, which you've worked so hard to build, is disheartening.

Elena Brennan is a shoe designer, and the founder and CEO of award-winning BUS STOP Boutique Inc, established in 2007 and headquartered in Philadelphia. She won Best International Business Woman in 2021. Since her journey as a shoe designer began, she has designed over thirty collections. Each collection is timeless, classic with a twist, and can be worn from the day into the night and from season to season. Above all, Elena's shoes are comfortable.

Elena's limited-edition shoe brand BUS STOP X launched in 2015 and is sold exclusively in her shop and on her website. She has led the company from a small boutique to an internationally recognised establishment. With a background in marketing and advertising, Elena is highly active in the Philadelphia region's economic development community. She serves on the boards of several organisations, including AIGA and SSHD Business Improvement District, and is an advisory committee member of Philadelphia Fashion Incubator and Support Philly Fashion – initiatives funded by Philadelphia City Council.

Born and raised in London, England, Elena was educated at the University of London. She resides in Philadelphia, in the US.

🌐 www.busstopboutique.com

in www.linkedin.com/in/elena-brennan-bus-stop-shoe-boutique

📷 www.instagram.com/busstopboutique

PART 4

Collaboration leads to long-term business success

CHAPTER 13

Win-Win

ENFYS MALONEY

You won't get far in business without harnessing the power, potential and possibilities that great collaboration brings. Or maybe you can, because of course you can succeed alone – but who would want that? I suppose it depends on your definition of success.

We all have an idea of what success looks like in our mind. For me, it is not standing alone on a high podium looking at what I've built and observing others from a distance; it is the opposite. True success is a togetherness; it is being alongside other ambitious women, running spectacular businesses, enjoying incredible experiences and meaningful, relationship-rich lives.

Success is not just about making great sales, it is also about the process of how those sales came about. For relationships, opportunities and excitement to blossom, you need to adopt a collaborative and creative approach when it comes to business development. As an individual and as a brand, collaboration is a way of life for me here at Sales Training with Enfys. It's how I've built my business, audience and reputation so quickly.

The women I support thrive because of the collective nature of how I deliver sales training. Having worked by themselves for many years, my clients feel a sense of relief and renewed confidence as they enter my programmes, which are designed to facilitate collaboration, friendship and long-lasting, fruitful business relationships.

Creating a new business model using collaboration

Collaboration, care and support are central to everything we do together within my business development mastermind, The Elevate Circle. Beyond the topics, sales training and many masterclasses I run, the connections and relationships my clients form provide the fuel that keeps their businesses moving. Not everything in business needs to be, or should be, purely for financial gain; your business can provide you with purpose, delivering impact as well as revenue. Great collaborations can help you to monetise your passion, create profit and delight your audience while also being meaningful and authentic to you and your brand.

It can be a strategic move to exchange something other than money, and if we boil it down, this is where the greatest collaborations come to life. True fulfilment in business comes from more than just making money, after all. You can boost your own business, and the businesses of others, by swapping services, sharing ideas, solving problems and working together for a common purpose. The reward and satisfaction you feel from being part of something is difficult to quantify but impossible to deny. Collaboration can be used to open doors to untold opportunities, experiences and conversations, and it can lead on to who knows what? It's an aspect of business-building that is not only enjoyable but can transform your organisation from the ordinary to the extraordinary, the exciting and the unexpected.

Using collaboration as a strategic tool to grow my audience has been invaluable to my business. I needed to establish myself as a voice in the industry, build credibility and get results quickly. One of the most effective things I've done has been to adopt a 'visibility strategy' alongside other, more established business owners. My business is designed as an ecosystem of collaboration, and my ethos as an individual and my approach to collaboration have been fundamental to my business success and rapid growth.

There are myriad examples I could share to illustrate this because the business I've built is a woven fabric of relationships, friendships and partnerships. I'd like to focus in particular on the idea of borrowing an audience to build my own, which has been fundamental to my success. It is not easy to build your audience, yet doing so is vital if you are to run a profitable, high-impact business. You cannot be the world's best-kept secret, but growing your audience alone is hard. Building your audience alongside other business owners and adopting a collaborative approach, however, can be a real joy that also produces incredible results.

Every business owner needs to grow their audience as it allows them to get their brand in front of new eyes and new prospects. For somebody to be interested in your business, you need to give them a reason to follow you. You need to consistently provide insightful, relevant and valuable content which draws your audience back to you again and again. By doing so, you actively nurture your followers, and your new prospects will step closer towards your offers or services each time they interact with your content. Sitting alongside your collaborators, you can position yourself as an expert in your industry; a credible brand worth listening to.

Your next clients need to buy into your brand before they buy from you, so it's vital that you establish trust. You need to provide social proof and demonstrate what your business stands for. To build my audience within The Business Lounge, my free Facebook group, I have been inviting well-established, well-respected business owners to talk to me. It's been a straightforward strategy as I've simply invited them into my free community and then promoted their brand in return. It's easy to overlook the power of invitation but it can work wonders; people hate feeling as if they are being sold to but love to be invited to things – so that's what I focused on doing.

Once I set up The Business Lounge community, I began to share a series of live talks – sessions that were designed to provide sales tips and inspire small business owners to build their businesses. I developed a crisp, beautiful and memorable brand for these talks, which soon became a tangible, well-respected element of my business. All of a sudden, I had an asset: a platform onto which I could invite other business owners to come and talk to me – a bit like an entrepreneurial talk show on Facebook.

By inviting other ambitious, interesting authors and business owners onto my Business Lounge Sofa, several things happened at once. My collaborators got the opportunity to promote their offering and display their expertise to my audience as I talked about, promoted and endorsed their work across all my channels. Being endorsed by me and my brand allowed them to build their own credibility, exposure and reputation.

At the same time, the same thing was happening to me. My new business was seen alongside some of the most well-known, well-respected names in the online business space. One of my guests has been on the front of Forbes, several are award-winning authors and others run well-known podcasts and publications. I won't lie: to begin with I was surprised that everybody I invited to speak to me on The Business Lounge Sofa said yes. The bigger the names I sat alongside, the bigger names I felt able to invite. It has been incredible. By consistently using the power of collaboration to grow my audience and proactively build my reputation, Sales Training with Enfys Ltd has become a well-regarded, award-winning, recognised business in a short amount of time. By boosting others, I simultaneously boosted my own brand and business. You can do the same.

Summary

To harness the power, potential and possibilities that collaboration can bring to your business, you need confidence, assertiveness and a boldness to suggest ideas beyond the obvious. You also need to ensure that each of you benefits from the arrangement. Great collaborations are always win-win. Any possibility that you could come away feeling like you pulled the short straw should be addressed before you proceed. Otherwise, you could end up feeling used, resentful and mistrusting of future opportunities.

TIPS FOR COLLABORATION

1. Be discerning

There are many ways to boost your brand with others. You can start small by inviting people to contribute within your space; they could provide a guest blog or you could invite them to talk to you online. A note of caution; not every collaboration is a good opportunity and not all will work out. Not everyone is as well-meaning as you are and you will need to learn when to say no and when to say yes to partnerships and strategic collaborations.

2. Aim for mutual benefit

Be clear on what you hope to gain from the arrangement and try to understand what the other person wants from you in return. Both parties need to get what they came for and it is absolutely OK to draft out the arrangement, expectations and time frames so you each understand what's involved and expected from the agreement. That said, most collaborations don't need such a formal plan and often come together organically as you speak and develop your ideas with your network and business circle.

3. Swap skills

Trading services can be especially prudent in the early days of building your business, when you may not have the funds to invest. A collaborative approach can allow you to get what you want by offering your services in exchange for whatever it is you need.

For example, in June I ran a high-profile workshop and I needed event photos and a photographer. I knew of one who wanted to attend, so we had a chat and traded services. I got some great event photos and she benefited from attending the sales strategy event for free. This was a simple and beneficial collaboration for both of us.

Collaboration can be simple one-offs or it can be a long-term arrangement that serves both parties. I've swapped group training sessions a couple of times this year, which worked brilliantly. My community benefited from email marketing training and my collaborator's community benefited from the sales strategy training I provided in return. We both gave something extra to our clients and we each got new clients from the traded sessions.

4. Be clear about your goals

Ask yourself what you want from your next collaboration. Who do you know who you'd love to do something with? Foster a curiosity and a confidence to see beyond the obvious and you will find an endless array of incredible opportunities hiding in the undiscovered realms of creative collaboration. Be assertive, be curious and go and experiment with your ideas.

5. Take the initiative

When you find business owners who share your passion, purpose and values, reach out and see what you can come up with. You can simply say to the next person you're drawn to, 'I'd love to collaborate with you someday' and see where it leads. Or you can be more direct, state what services you'd like to swap and ask if they'd be interested. Whatever you go on to do, enjoy the process of building your business and the kaleidoscope of opportunities that great win-win collaborations can bring; there is nothing better.

Enfys Maloney helps business owners to achieve more in less time and ultimately to enjoy more sales, more profit, more fulfilment, more confidence and more reward from their businesses. Sales Training with Enfys helps women galvanise their earnings and bring in consistent, reliable revenue.

Enfys has supported hundreds of women with their sales. Her collaborative sales strategy is not only a cornerstone of her own success but also of the success of her many clients. The Elevate Circle is Enfys' high-level business development mastermind, which enables ambitious businesswomen to generate high-revenue months, every month. Join Enfys' vibrant sales training group, The Business Lounge, for free on Facebook or connect with her on LinkedIn today.

🌐 www.salestrainingwithenfys.co.uk

in www.linkedin.com/in/withenfys

🔲 www.instagram.com/salestraining_with_enfys

CHAPTER 14

Collaboration Unpacked

HELA WOZNIAK-KAY

There's an African saying that rings in my ears when I think of collaboration: 'If you want to go fast, go alone. If you want to go far, go together.'

Going Solo: Many moons ago I was invited to celebrate a remarkable woman who'd made her mark in the history books, and make the case for the indelible signature she'd left on the landscape. The brief was to step into her shoes in front of an audience and share her story. The shoes I was invited to wear were those of aviatrix Amy Johnson, Queen of the Air, who gained worldwide recognition by flying solo from Croydon to Darwin in a de Havilland Gipsy Moth. She took off from Croydon Airport on 5 May 1930 and landed in Darwin, Australia nineteen days later. Hats off to Amy. What an achievement by one individual flying solo, although I've often wondered what history would have made of her achievement had she been a double act.

Two to Tango: It takes two to tango, and I first experienced the exquisite epitome of a double act at the Southbank Centre in London over ten years ago, in the form of two amateur aficionados of the Argentine tango – the double-bubble duo, Annabel and Clive. I can still picture their symbiosis and utter unity, which took my breath away. They were totally in tune with each other and utterly in sync. It was the perfect collaboration *à deux* and resulted in a mesmerising performance.

Collaboration is a Dance: Before thinking about whether collaboration is your jam, think about whether you're Amy, or Annabel looking to find a Clive. Or a collective of Clives. Then decide on your preferred boogie-woogie: tango, waltz, rumba or samba, cha-cha-cha or jitterbug. Perhaps you want to be part of a bigger performance, such as the Saturday Night Fever Brooklyn Shuffle or Los del Río's Macarena. Or you want to become a zombie and join in with Thrill The World, an annual global tribute to seasonal ghoulishness that celebrates the memory of the multi-talented 'King of Pop' Michael Jackson by gathering to perform 'Thriller'.

Co-operate or Collaborate: The heart of co-operation rests in sharing ideas. Collaboration, on the other hand, generates ideas. It sparks innovation. It can lead to delicious disruption in a sector, or open the door to a new way of thinking.

Everybody Wins: Collaboration is a gateway to unique perspectives and experiences. Collaborators gravitate for a common purpose and generously share knowledge, know-how, skills and experience. This is collaborative harmony where everybody wins, and the foundations are trust, truth, shared values and freedom of speech.

Put on Your Red Shoes and Dance the Blues: The business world can be competitive and harsh. While competition is unavoidable and can create separation, there are endless opportunities to collaborate with other businesses, brands and individuals to diversify your audience, reach new customers, improve products and enhance services. If you choose wisely, collaboration can solve problems and achieve goals that seem to be out of reach when working alone.

When collaborators are in tune, a set of hormones come out to play. Say hello to let's-get-this-party-started dopamine. Welcome the proud-as-punch hormone serotonin. Get a hit of those wellbeing endorphins and the moral molecule oxytocin, also known as the love or cuddle hormone. A honey pot of trust, love and bonding. The cornerstones of collaboration.

Reaching far and wide through collaboration

Brandlicious Brand You: When my first copy of *Brand You Magazine* landed, I did a little dance as I devoured the contagious content contained in each page. A chocolate box full of wisdom, insight and stories from a host of fabulous female entrepreneurs. The magazine itself is a collaborative endeavour, a one-stop destination for female business owners around the globe. It celebrates a world where businesswomen are empowered to shimmy out of the shadows and be fearless in their pursuit of creating successful businesses and brands. It provides inspiration from women who have boldly designed a business and lifestyle they always craved.

Because I was head over heels in love with *Brand You*, I desired a Sister Snog limited edition. One that told the story of a brand that was celebrating two decades of connecting remarkable businesswomen, and that would be given out to all the past, present and future Sisters who came to celebrate in their bright and brilliant brand hues at an afternoon tea in London Town.

The event was a confectionery connoisseurs' collaboration between The Chesterfield and Hardys Sweet Shop that took guests on a nostalgic trip rediscovering old favourites and presented them with the thrill of discovering something new and scrumptious. The limited edition told the story of Sister Snog: The business. The brand. The Yin and Yang of the founders. It featured members and painted a picture of Sisterliness. It was an Argentine tango between two brand owners who worked in harmony to create something original and individual. Every *Brand You* edition has a theme; Sister Snog's was utterly BRANDLIOUS.

The Soulful Concert: Over the years, Sister Snog has explored many different avenues of connectivity and collaboration with its members. One that brought Sisters together in pure harmony was Sisters of Soul: a choir that united those who wanted to sing. Group singing is an excellent icebreaker that helps forge social bonds, enhances a state of happiness and creates a strong sense of wellbeing as those playful hormones kick in. The beauty of Sisters of Soul was that there were no auditions. Everyone who was a member of the Tribe was welcome. The debut performance was at a Festive Friday with a backdrop of Swarovski Crystals, Christmas Cocktails and Canapés.

Although the choir only had a repertoire of three songs, that was no barrier to the idea of hosting a concert, but a reality check highlighted the fact that three sets probably didn't quite make the grade for a night to remember. Thanks to Lynne Parker, founder and CEO of Funny Women and a Soul Sister, before we knew it the London Gay Men's Chorus was part of the repertoire. They opened the door to a collective of West End starlets who sang as Eden Voices when they weren't performing, then All The King's Men, King's College London's all-male a cappella group, squared the circle. Ukulele Lady, aka Sara Spade, joined the dots and added a ray of sunshine to the performance.

The concert was held at St Bride's, one of the most fascinating historic churches in London, renowned for outstanding music and, if rumours are to be believed, its spire, which was the inspiration behind the traditional wedding cake.

Katie Piper OBE was the star guest and we raised a pot of cash for the Katie Piper Foundation. The evening was pure magic Brooklyn Shuffle. A harmonious collaboration united by a shared love of singing.

A Signature Scent: Sisterliness is nothing like you expected yet everything you were looking for. It's a combination of intricately woven values, a set of brand beliefs, distinctive personality traits and a palette of hues, tones and flavours. The Sister Snog brand colour palette is made up of seven shades of purple: semi-precious and sensuous amethyst; dark and mysterious aubergine; lavender with its cool hue and tint of blue; lilac, lazy-hazy and full of playtime; delicious plum with berry tones; ultra-light, uber-sharp violet; and wisteria, which personifies a soft power that's gentle and oriental.

The sense of smell is a powerful trigger, and all scents tell their own narrative. They are evocative, and can be memory triggers that lead to an emotional response or a trip down memory lane. There are many ways to grow and nurture a distinctive brand. Creating a signature scent that speaks without saying a word is one of them. Combining the hallmark of Sisterliness with elements of the colour palette formed the basis of a fragrant collaboration between yours truly and Jo Tocher, founder of Essences by Jo. Jo is an essence mixologist, something of an alchemist as well as a qualified aromatherapist.

We spent an afternoon together mixing, blending, refining until the Essence of Sisterliness was captured, bottled and gifted to Sisters at a Wonderful-One-Off in-person event. This was an example of a Viennese waltz-type collaboration where we stirred clockwise and counterclockwise until the blend was complete.

Power of the Pack: Apparently, women release more oxytocin than men. That's not to say men don't make perfect collaborators; of course they do. Consider for a moment some of the big ideas that have changed the world and been driven by some rather cool dudes: the Wright brothers delivered the aeroplane; John Lennon and Paul McCartney changed popular music forever; Steve Jobs and Steve Wozniak invented Apple computers; Larry Page and Sergey Brin started a company that would later become Google. But there's something extra potent in the power of the pack. When women reach out in their quest to collaborate with each other, build circles of trust, put on their red shoes and dance the blues, they release the potency of female power to create mind-boggling impact.

If you haven't seen the film *The Woman King*, which is about the Agojie, an all-female warrior unit that protected the West African kingdom of Dahomey from the seventeenth to the nineteenth centuries, put it on your list. Or dip into the legend of the Amazonian women. Women who wore trousers, smoked pot, embellished their skin with tattoos, rode horses, cut off their right breasts so they could fire bows with utter accuracy and fought as hard as the guys.

Summary

The modern workplace is somewhat of a paradox. On the one hand, it's become more dispersed. On the other, it's more connected than ever before – which means there'll be a place or platform or party that has your name on it. Dip in, dip out until you find the one that works for you, whether that's online or in-person or a combination of both. You are the company you keep. Choose wisely. Once you've found a community and support network of cheerleaders and champions, you'll find your collaborators. Then choose whether you want to tango, waltz or do the Brooklyn Shuffle.

TIPS FOR COLLABORATION

1. Work in harmony

Collaboration is the ultimate intertwining of skills, passion and knowledge to concoct the most shatterproof forms of changemaking. Working in collaborative harmony means there's no leader. Everyone has a right to be heard and listened to. Differences should be resolved collectively and voices heard individually. Successful collaboration requires a common purpose, emotional engagement, freedom of speech, candour, mutual respect and open negotiation.

2. Don't collaborate with a stranger

Finding a pool of potential collaborators is a quest. Think of Jason and his search for the golden fleece with his gang of Argonauts. Become an Argonautette. Join a tribe of giant thinkers ready to catapult their businesses to new levels by harnessing the power of a club or collective that's full of community spirit with a tribal culture.

Hela Wozniak-Kay is The Connectress, a charismatic catalyst who connects remarkable businesswomen brimming with entrepreneurial spirit. She's also the soul of a power brand led by women for women: Sister Snog. It is an ecosystem where like-minded go-getters support each other so they can continue to thrive, boost their bottom line, supercharge their business and invigorate their brand, one sparkling connection at a time.

Hela is in daily contact with a cross section of businesswomen so she understands the challenges small business owners face and conquer on a daily basis. In Hela's world, connections are today's golden currency. That's why she believes everyone should find their tribe and join it.

Thank you to all the Sisters, Big Sisters and Really Big Sisters who took a leap of faith to be part of *Fab Collab*.

And Mindy for being the catalyst and Book Midwife® who made sure we collaborated to create a symphony of Sisterliness.

🌐 www.sistersnog.com

💼 www.linkedin.com/in/hela-wozniak-kay

📷 www.instagram.com/sistersnog

📷 www.instagram.com/totallyhela

CHAPTER 15

The Legacy Of Collaboration

DEBBIE GILBERT

Collaboration is about building a solid network of people with whom you have synergy, and who share your vision, goals and strategy. My journey to becoming a successful collaborator began at age seven as a Brownie, when I learnt the value of teamwork. It has been key to my business success: I have developed a successful marketing and events agency supporting a wide range of businesses.

Being a business owner is a long way off from my long career in the travel industry. The travel business took me to some fantastic places, and every day was enjoyable. Working together as a team was vital to get a job done well. Life changed dramatically after I had my son in 1994. My husband and I separated while I was pregnant, so I had to return to work full-time when my son was seventeen weeks old. Life became a constant juggle of work and motherhood. I tried to cope with a demanding role for two years, working long hours. It was exhausting.

The decision to leave in 1997 was difficult, but with no family support close by, I relocated back to Hertfordshire to be near my family. Shortly afterwards, my father was diagnosed with early-onset dementia, meaning my parents needed help. If I'd had support and people around me, maybe my life would have taken a different path. Setting up a business so I could work around my family seemed the most logical option, so in 1998, way before the internet and social media, and due to the circumstances I faced at the time, my business started by accident.

During that time, life running a business was lonely. There was little in the way of networking events or support. In 2004 I joined the newly launched Women in Business Network and soon realised that building a supportive network would help me build my business. After a brief stint as a franchisee with Women on Top in 2009, I launched my own networking company, which was a game changer for me.

Connecting people who could collaborate came naturally to me; I could see potential in joint ventures others had missed. Watching the magic of businesses working together, sometimes from the same industry, is tremendously satisfying. Working with others can be challenging, but if the combination of skills and personality types is right, it can be dynamite. I am well known for working with and supporting others; as a result good things always come back to me.

Building a business is tough; from a sole trader to a large company, it comes with challenges. Finding a way to work with others harmoniously is vital, and not everyone finds this task a breeze. We often hear the expressions 'stay in your lane' or 'don't speak to competitors' but this is terrible advice. Collaboration is intrinsic to business success; it is the glue that cements the business to clients, fellow business owners and the community. Businesses struggle to survive if they don't collaborate.

The long-term benefits of collaboration

Back in 2014, collaboration helped me to set up The Best Businesswomen Awards, one of the most successful female business awards in the UK. As a solopreneur with a small team, I knew this could only work if I pulled people in to judge and sponsor the project, and help me promote it.

I drew up a list of who could potentially sponsor and who would make a good judge. Then I built a second list of people I knew with large female networks that could help me share the news. I also needed a place to hold a launch party, a venue for the final, a photographer and a videographer. The next step was approaching these people and seeing if I could get their buy-in. Two venues were on my list: one where I held regular events already and knew would be ideal for the launch party; the other I had never used, but it was local and I knew the events manager. Both said yes immediately.

I explained to them that the events might not go ahead if I didn't get anyone interested. They were supportive and agreed to hold the dates without payment until a month before the final – unheard of in the events world. This showed their belief in me and their faith in this collaboration. Part of the deal was they would get free sponsorship.

The next task was to draw up the first year's budget; honestly, it was all guesswork. Then we worked on preparing a sponsor's pack and the judge's brief. With trepidation, I picked up the phone. I had known Sharon Montgomery from Crane and Staples Solicitors for some time. I knew they were big fans of awards. Sharon was that first phone call, something I will never forget. The conversation began, 'Hi Sharon, I am setting up business awards for women and wondered if Crane and Staples would sponsor?' Sharon replied, 'For Hertfordshire?' I explained that it would be the whole of the UK. She said, 'Wow, what a task – well, count us in. I am sure you will make it a great success.'

This immediate confirmation that they would not only sponsor but join the judging panel and be part of the awards gave me a huge confidence boost. The next few days were spent calling people – I didn't bother with emails. I knew that for this to work, I had to pick up the phone; it was key that people heard my enthusiasm and excitement. Gradually, over a week or so, I signed up ten sponsors and eight judges. The biggest thing for me was that no one said no. This was because, over the years, I had built those foundations and people knew not only who I was but that I could collaborate and deliver.

Over time the awards have grown, and people approach me each year to be involved. I am also constantly thinking about who else I can collaborate with. I know being part of this makes a real difference to my sponsors and judges. It's a profile raiser, a great way to build their networks and put their names to something exceptional. There is nothing better than celebrating success.

In 2011 I launched a networking company called Mums UnLtd, recently rebranded to Businesswomen UnLtd. This was aimed at mums who were starting a business and needed support and advice. From that first group, people came to me and asked if they could launch a group in their area. I knew that help was needed far and wide, so I put together some training and offered this to others on a profit-sharing basis. It has been a fabulous way to collaborate with other female entrepreneurs, and watching the fantastic transformations in their lives has been wonderful. Each time I visit one of the groups and hear success stories of collaboration, sharing and the difference our groups have made, it is hugely satisfying. Some great examples are therapists who have combined skills to offer workshops to their clients, marketing consultants linking with SEO experts, website designers collaborating with graphic designers – the list goes on and on.

The 3 Counties Expo is my other long-term significant collaboration. Born from an idea to gather businesses together from Hertfordshire, Bedfordshire and Buckinghamshire, I approached two key female entrepreneurs, one operating in Bedfordshire and the other in Hertfordshire. We worked together for four consecutive years (until Covid came along) and created well-attended, annual events in Luton, Bedford and Watford. Without collaborating, this event simply would not have happened. We pooled our email list and resources and split the profits, taking on equal shares of the work involved.

Summary

This world was built on collaboration; without it, we simply would not have the structure we have in society today. To be successful in business, you must find ways to collaborate with others; no woman is an island. Spending time finding successful partners, people you can learn from and support, will create a legacy. It is time well spent. Over the years, not all collaborations have worked but, like most things we try that do not work, we learn from them.

TIPS FOR COLLABORATION

1. Make sure there is chemistry

If you want to work with someone, you must ensure the chemistry is there. It is like any relationship, and they must share your vision and outcomes for the project. Finding people with skills you don't have can work well, but you need an understanding of what they do and how they work. Discuss the collaboration thoroughly; spending lots of time on this will save any issues later.

2. Trust your gut

From your initial discussion, and you might need more than one meeting, you can ascertain if the collaboration is going to work for you. Sometimes at this stage, I have politely walked away. This could be for several reasons; usually, something just didn't feel right. Trust your gut; it's rarely wrong. Lots of people, almost weekly, approach me to collaborate with them on a variety of projects. I consider carefully how this will benefit my business.

3. Allocate time wisely

Time is precious, so don't overcommit to lots of collaborations that will eat into the time you could be spending growing your business in other ways or with family or friends.

Before undertaking any collaboration, set clear boundaries. Who will do what tasks? An understanding of what each person brings to the table is vital and you should decide how you will communicate. Some collaborations will be a one-off project, some will be long-term.

4. Do your research

If you are thinking about running an event and want to collaborate with another, look deeply into their online reputation, their social media following and their email list, and act with due diligence. I have seen people get involved with someone who didn't have an excellent reputation and ultimately damaged their business. Events are one of the key areas that can work well as a collaboration project. Find people with a similar demographic to your clients and share the costs and workload. This will be mutually beneficial.

5. Reach out

Seek out and discover collaborations from networking events and LinkedIn. Write a wish list of the types of businesses you want to collaborate with. Then, reach out; the worst thing they can say to you is no. From an initial discussion, they might know others they want to involve or to whom they can refer you.

Be clear about what your aims and goals of the collaboration are and articulate what the benefits will be.

Debbie Gilbert is a multi-award-winning entrepreneur and owner of Viva Business Support, a marketing and events agency. She is also the founder of The Best Businesswomen Awards and Businesswomen UnLtd. Her book *The Successful Mumpreneur*, which shares her knowledge on growing a business around a family, has been a global success.

Over the past twenty years, Debbie has built a reputation for being a queen of collaboration and an excellent supporter of small businesses and start-ups. Growing a solid network has been her priority, and integral to her business success. Her motto is, 'When you reach the top of your mountain, throw down a rope and help someone else up.'

🌐 www.vivabusinesssupport.co.uk

🌐 www.businesswomenunltd.co.uk

🌐 www.bestbusinesswomenawards.com